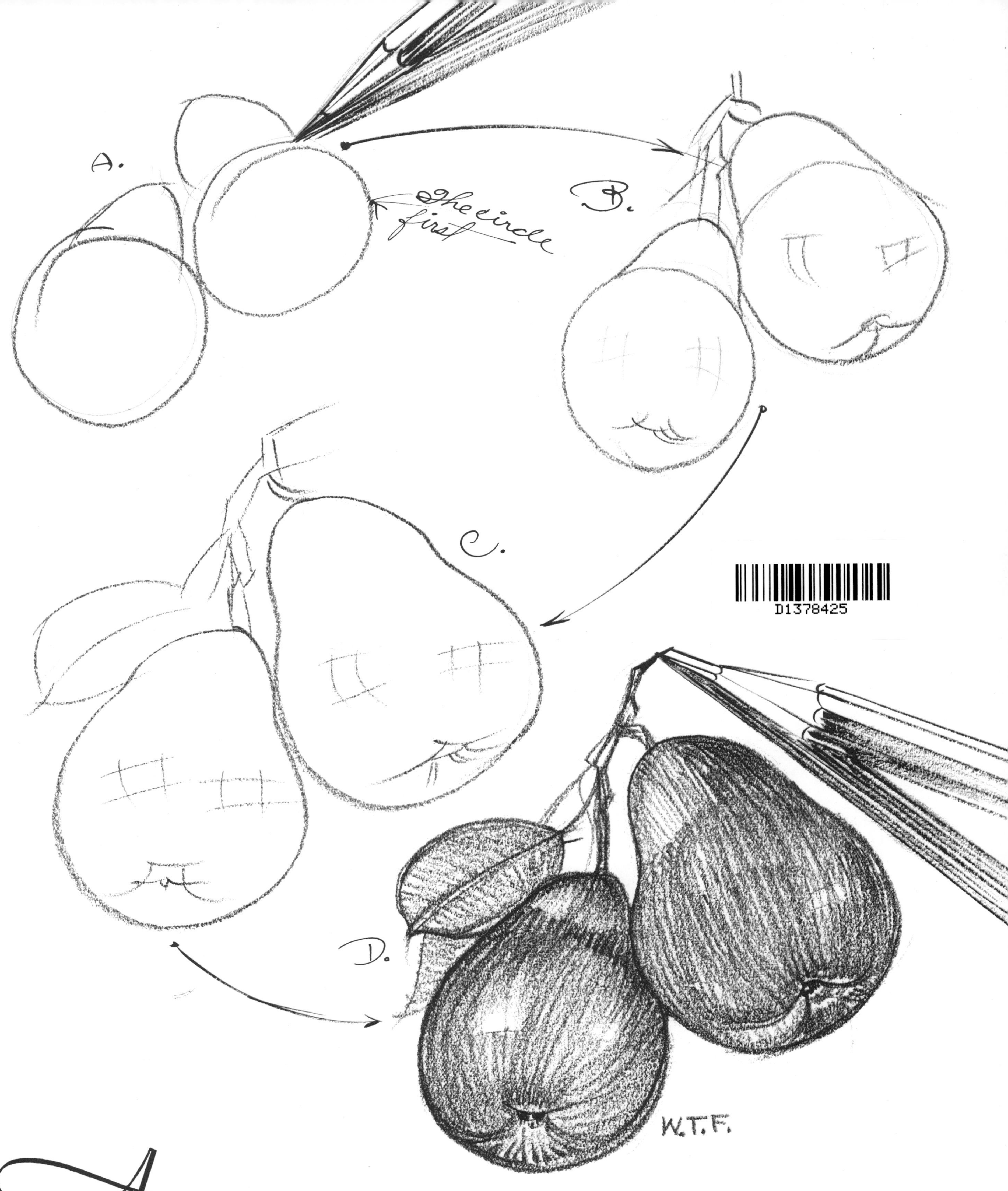

Again we have the circle to build on with an added half-oval for the upper part of the pear. Now, if you have a good outline as in C, proceed to shade, leaving the highlights. They are the part that gives you roundness and shine. Note the way the lines go with the form of the pear. After trying this try drawing the same from fruit you may have. This is wonderful practice. Never think that *anything* you do with mind or hands is lost motion especially your mistakes as it makes you a much better workman. This is what makes an experienced practitioner whether in the arts or around home.

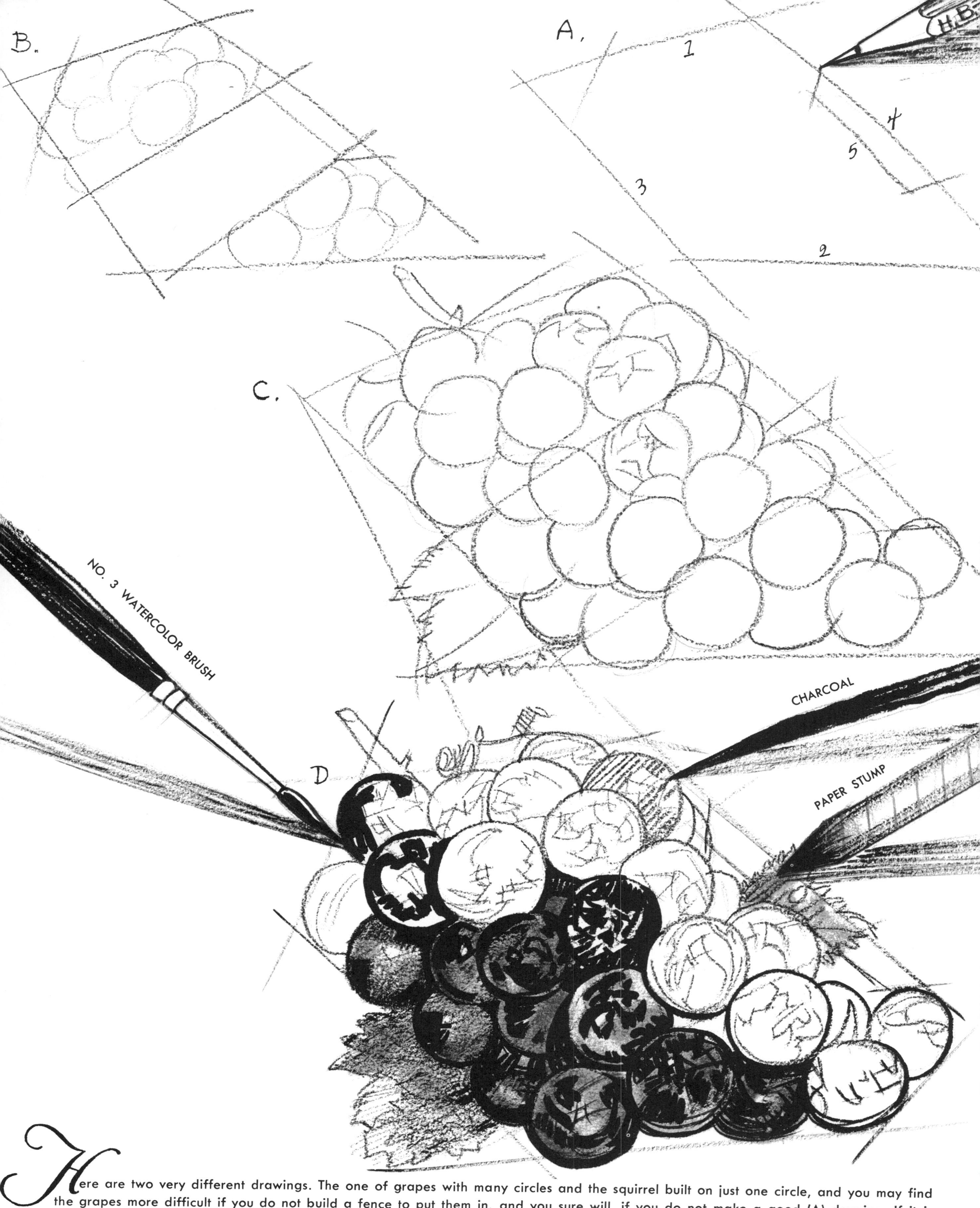

Here are two very different drawings. The one of grapes with many circles and the squirrel built on just one circle, and you may find the grapes more difficult if you do not build a fence to put them in, and you sure will, if you do not make a good (A) drawing. If it is right, all the circles or grapes will fall right in place. You will find it well worth your time to think while, and before you start to work on this drawing. This is blocked in with pencil. You can use charcoal if you wish, and finish with charcoal and paper stump. The solid blacks with No. 3 water color brushes and India ink.

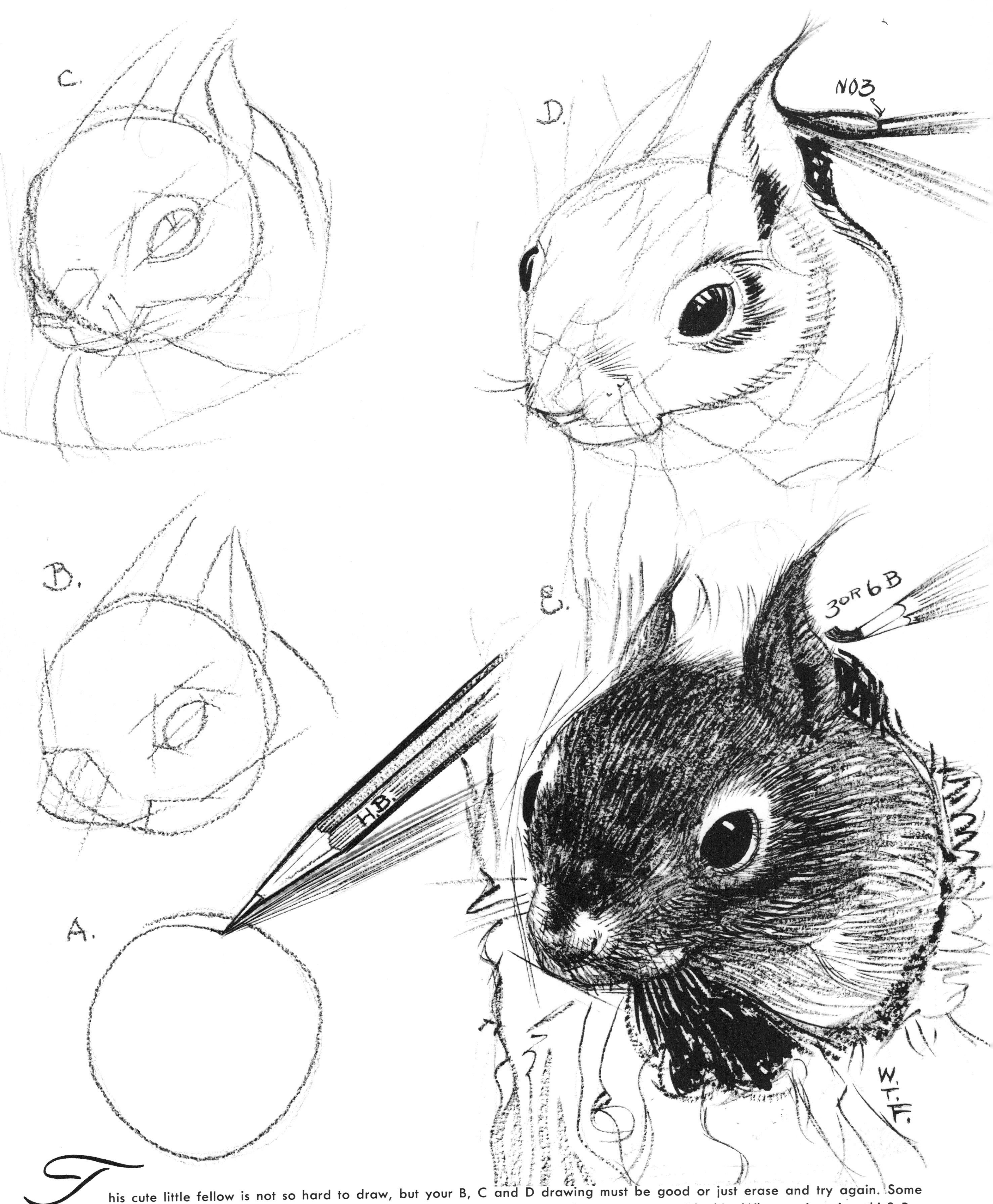

This cute little fellow is not so hard to draw, but your B, C and D drawing must be good or just erase and try again. Sometimes drawing comes out easy and good, other times not so good, so one learns to cope with this. Why am I saying this? Because it just happened to me. I started the day with a horse head I had sketched in, and it looked like it would be very easy. Well, it wasn't, and I spoiled it. So, to change my luck, I started on this drawing. It rolled along — no trouble at all. What am I going to do with the horse drawing? Make it over and over until I have just what I want. Remember, you do the same, if it happens to you.

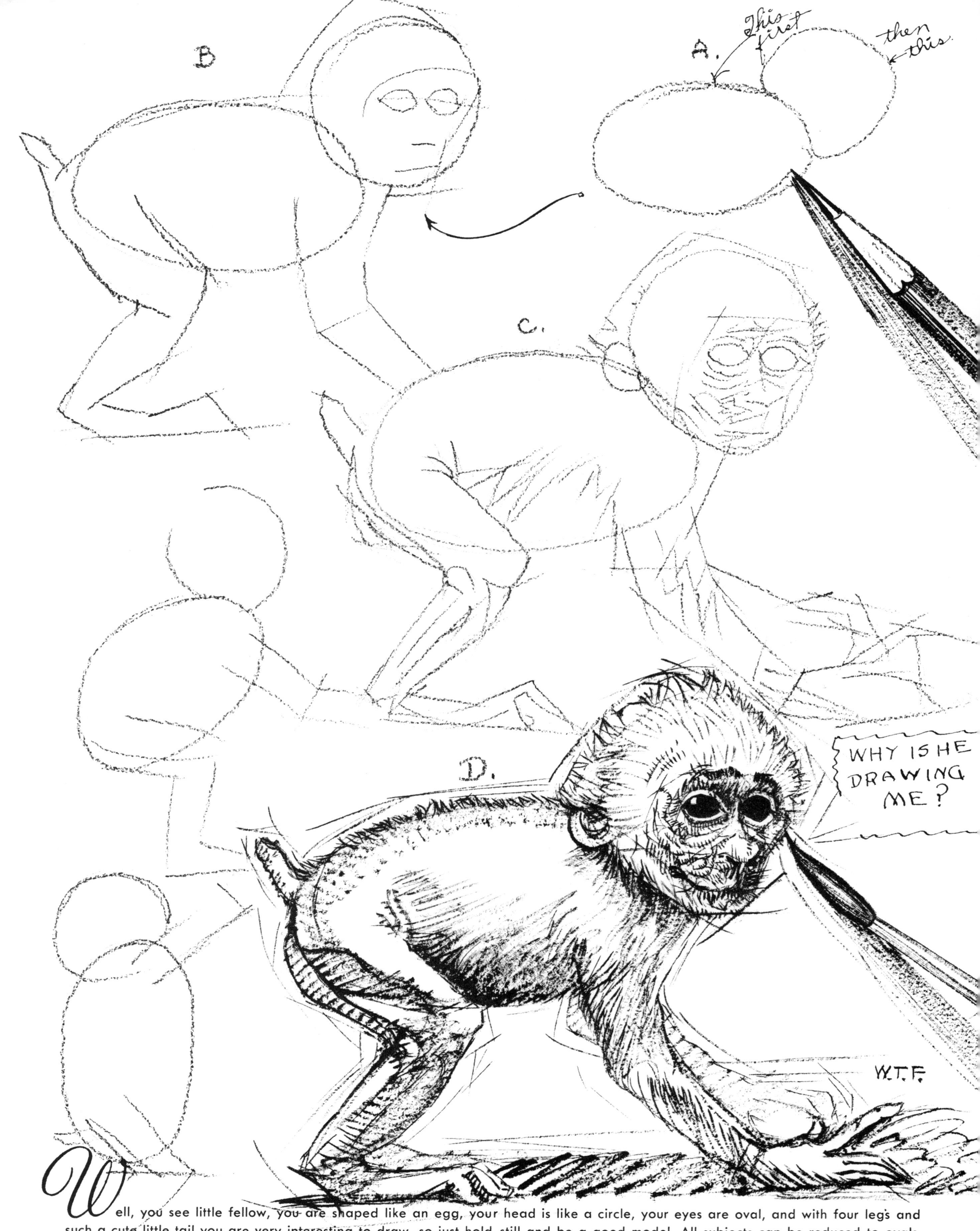

Well, you see little fellow, you are shaped like an egg, your head is like a circle, your eyes are oval, and with four legs and such a cute little tail you are very interesting to draw, so just hold still and be a good model. All subjects can be reduced to ovals, circles, oblongs or squares, so learn to think and see things in simple forms. It will help you draw well much sooner. Baby animals are one of my favorite subjects and if you can draw life into them it is a lot of satisfaction and you will not have too much trouble drawing many things.

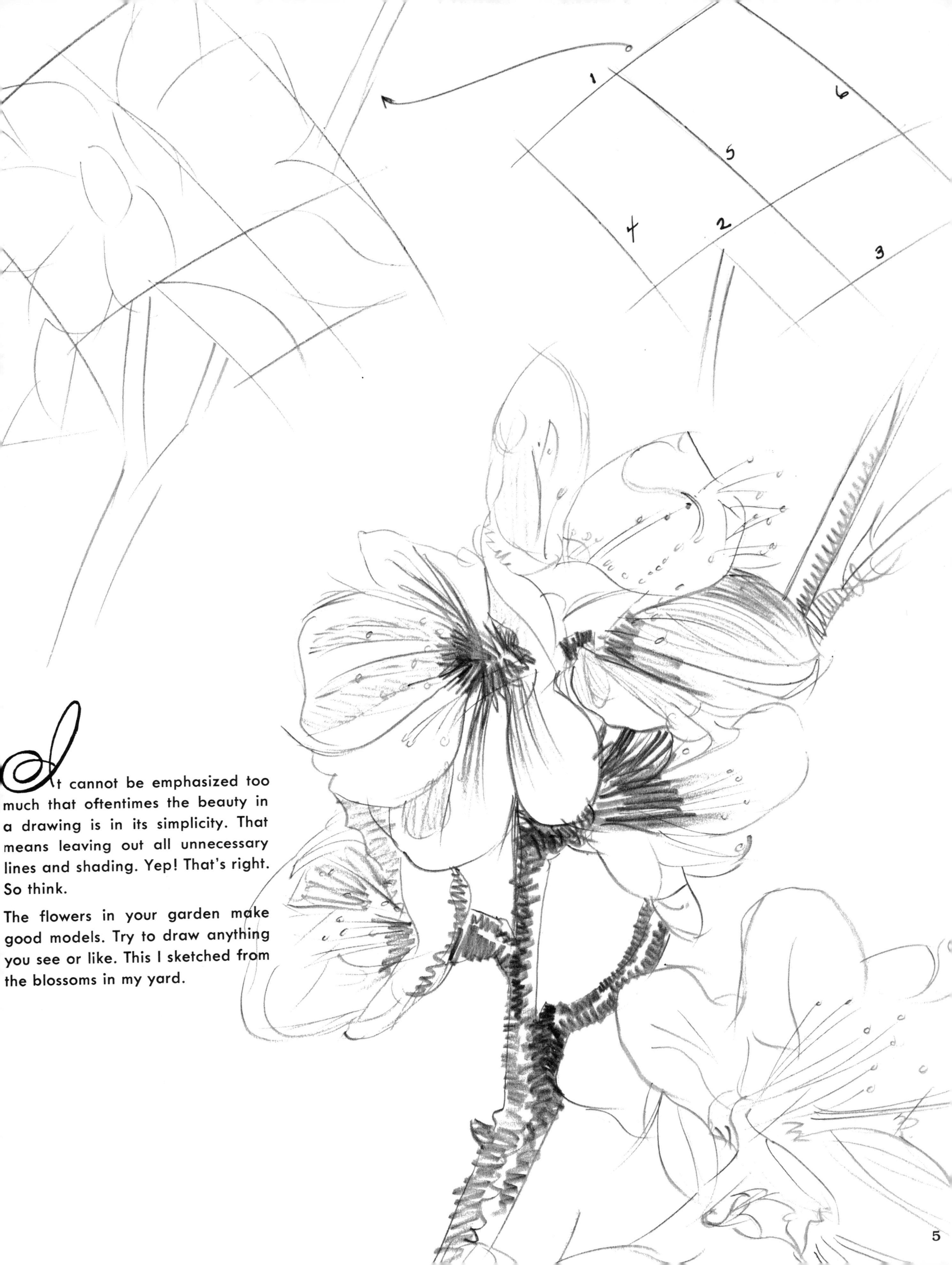

It cannot be emphasized too much that oftentimes the beauty in a drawing is in its simplicity. That means leaving out all unnecessary lines and shading. Yep! That's right. So think.

The flowers in your garden make good models. Try to draw anything you see or like. This I sketched from the blossoms in my yard.

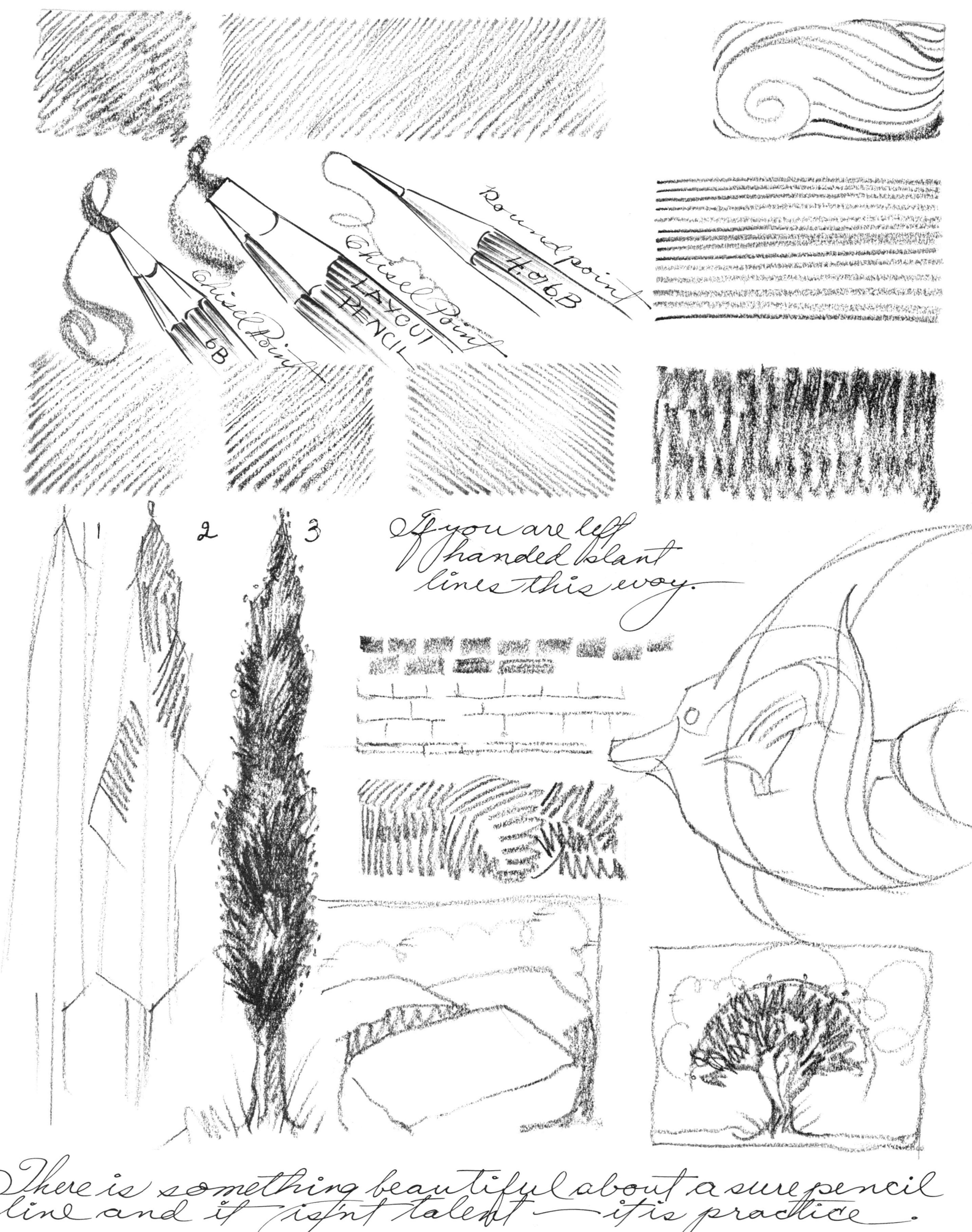

There is something beautiful about a sure pencil line and it isn't talent — it is practice.

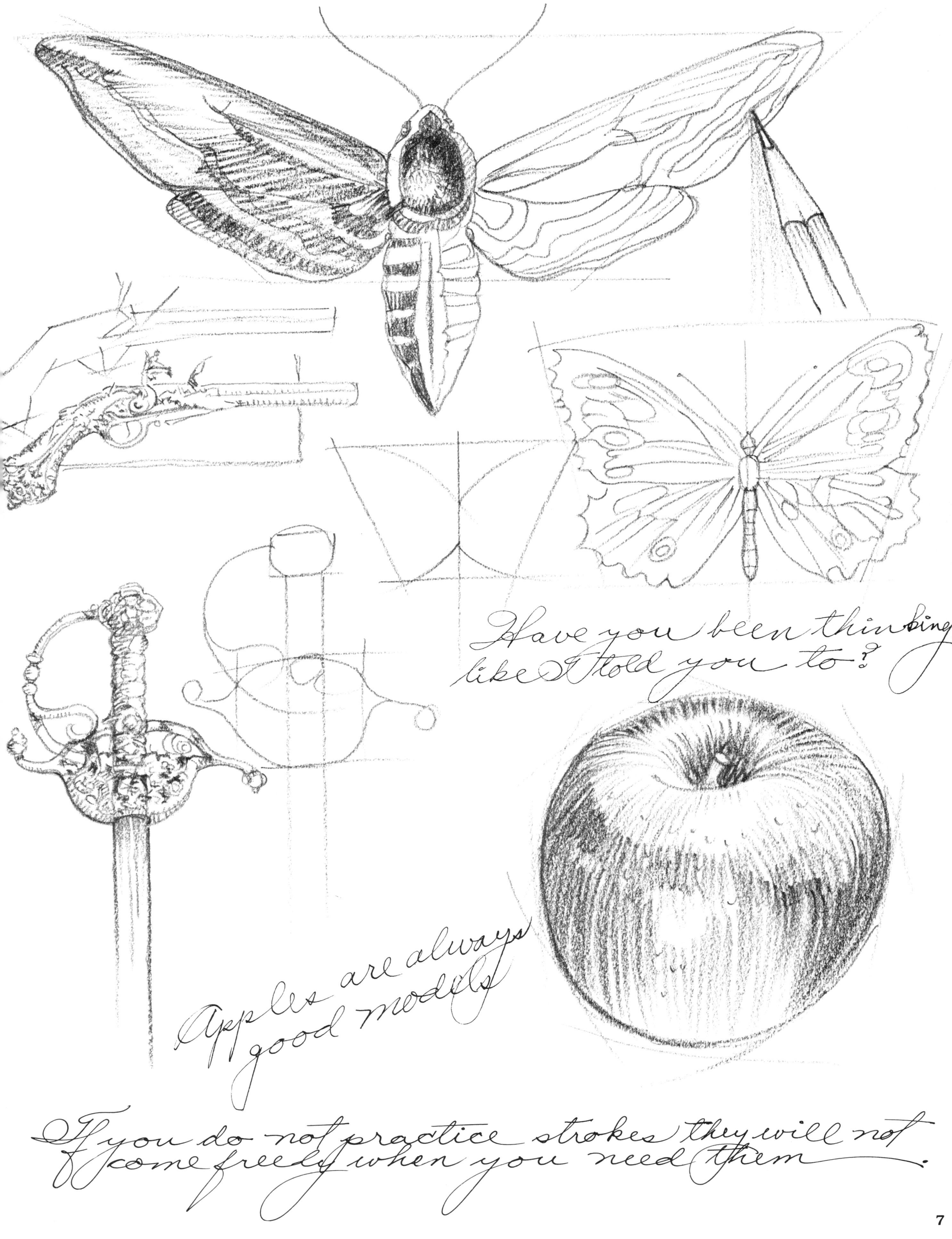
Have you been thinking like I told you to?
Apples are always good models
If you do not practice strokes they will not come freely when you need them.

THE USE OF PEN AND INK

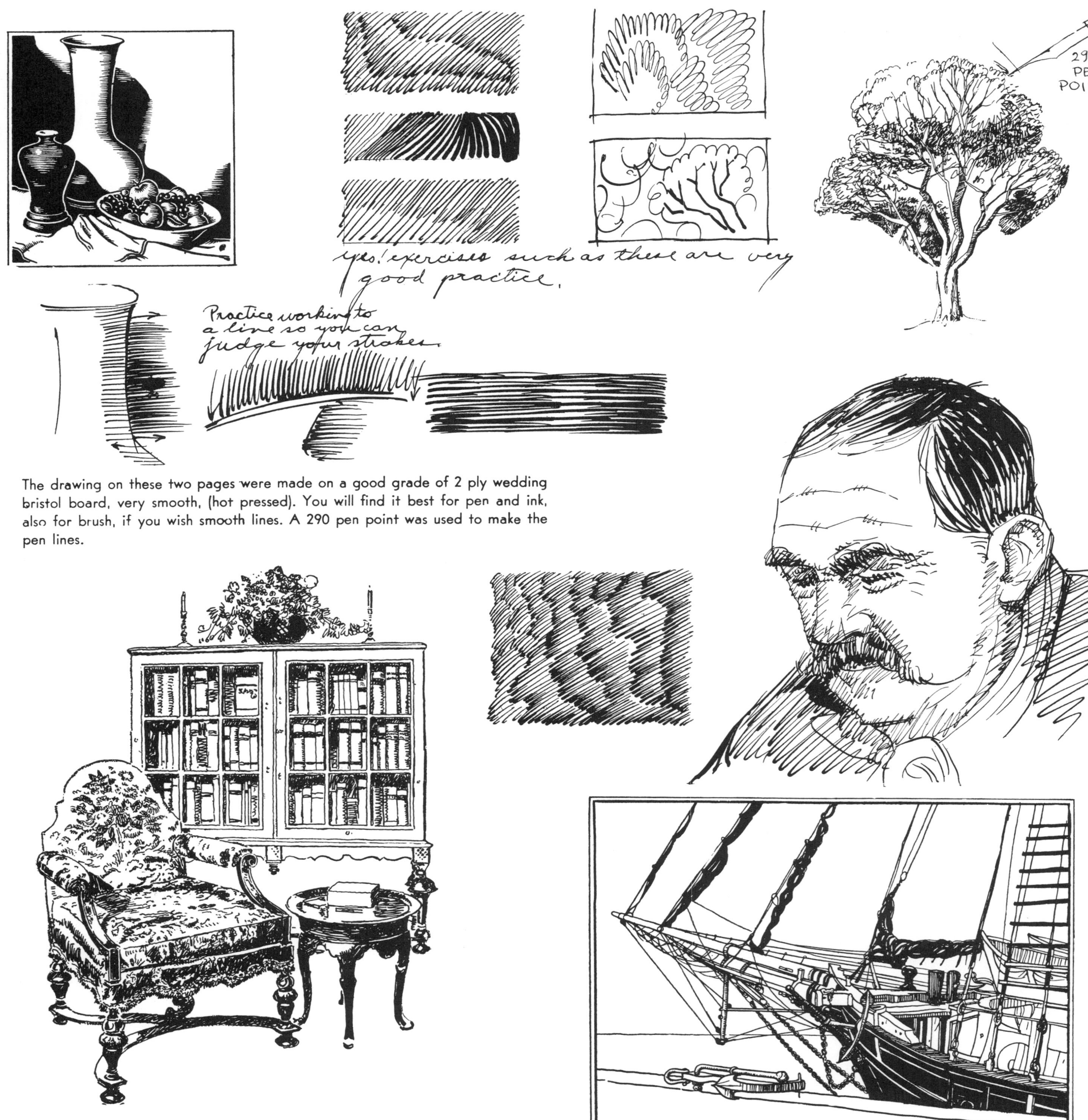

The drawing on these two pages were made on a good grade of 2 ply wedding bristol board, very smooth, (hot pressed). You will find it best for pen and ink, also for brush, if you wish smooth lines. A 290 pen point was used to make the pen lines.

TERRE-NEUVA "ROUZIC" AT SAINT-SERVAN

WHEN working on a pen and ink or brush drawing, always block in and round out your drawing first, with H.B. pencil. I like one ot the mechanical pencils and sharpen lead to point on sandpaper —much quicker and cleaner. The 290 pen point is quite tricky to start with. It is very flexible and will make a fine line as well as broad strokes. A 170 pen point, writing pen or your fountain pen, is fine. Be sure to ink in with a good black if you wish to have it published.

THE USE OF BRUSH AND INK

Hold your brush free and easy with arm on drawing board. For fine lines hold brush vertical from paper and use arm movement.

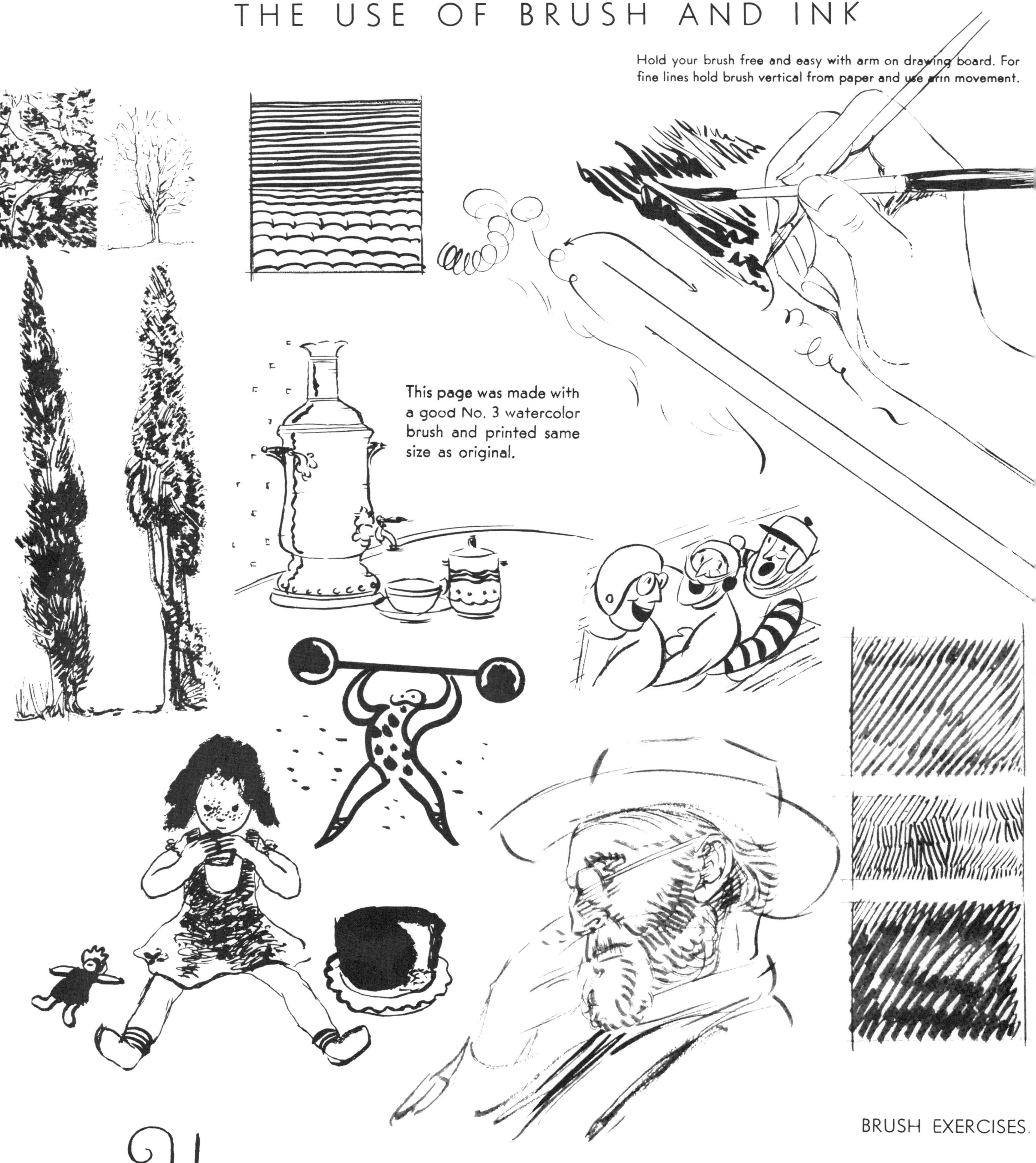

This page was made with a good No. 3 watercolor brush and printed same size as original.

BRUSH EXERCISES.

YOU can obtain different effects by using paper with rough or grained surfaces. Use brush slightly dry. The paper you like best will only be decided upon by trying them all. Practice, practice and enjoy it. Good going.

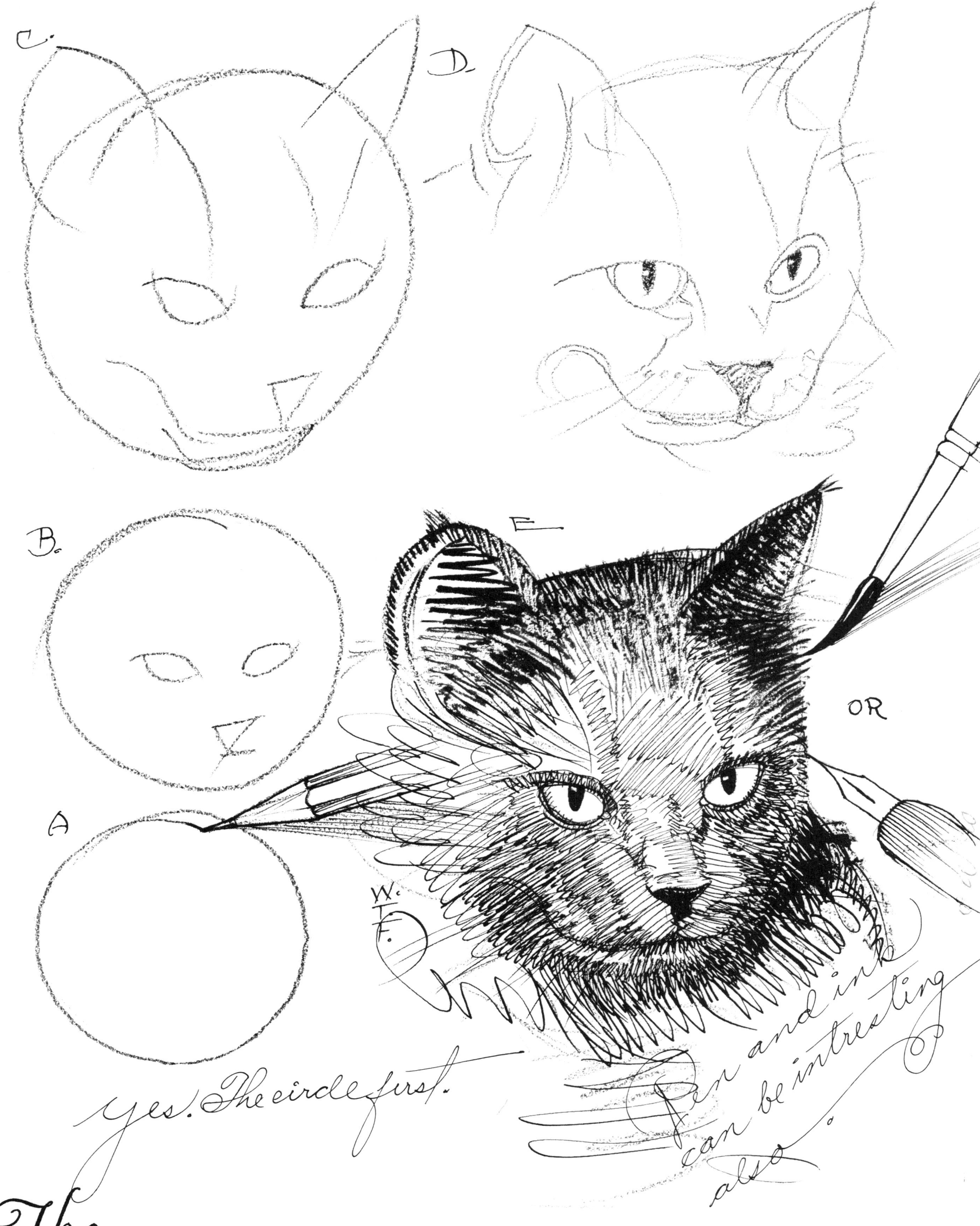

The cat, like all all other round-faced animals, can be built on a circle, but don't do like a student of mine did years ago when I gave private lessons. She had made a drawing of a cow's head on one of my charts made for the human head only. I told her in fun as the cow's head was not too good, "You know, Mrs.............. you have accomplished something I never thought possible, something I have never been able to do." She said, "I have?" So always use just good old common sense and you will come out much better. I think you will like drawing this cat and dog. Good going!

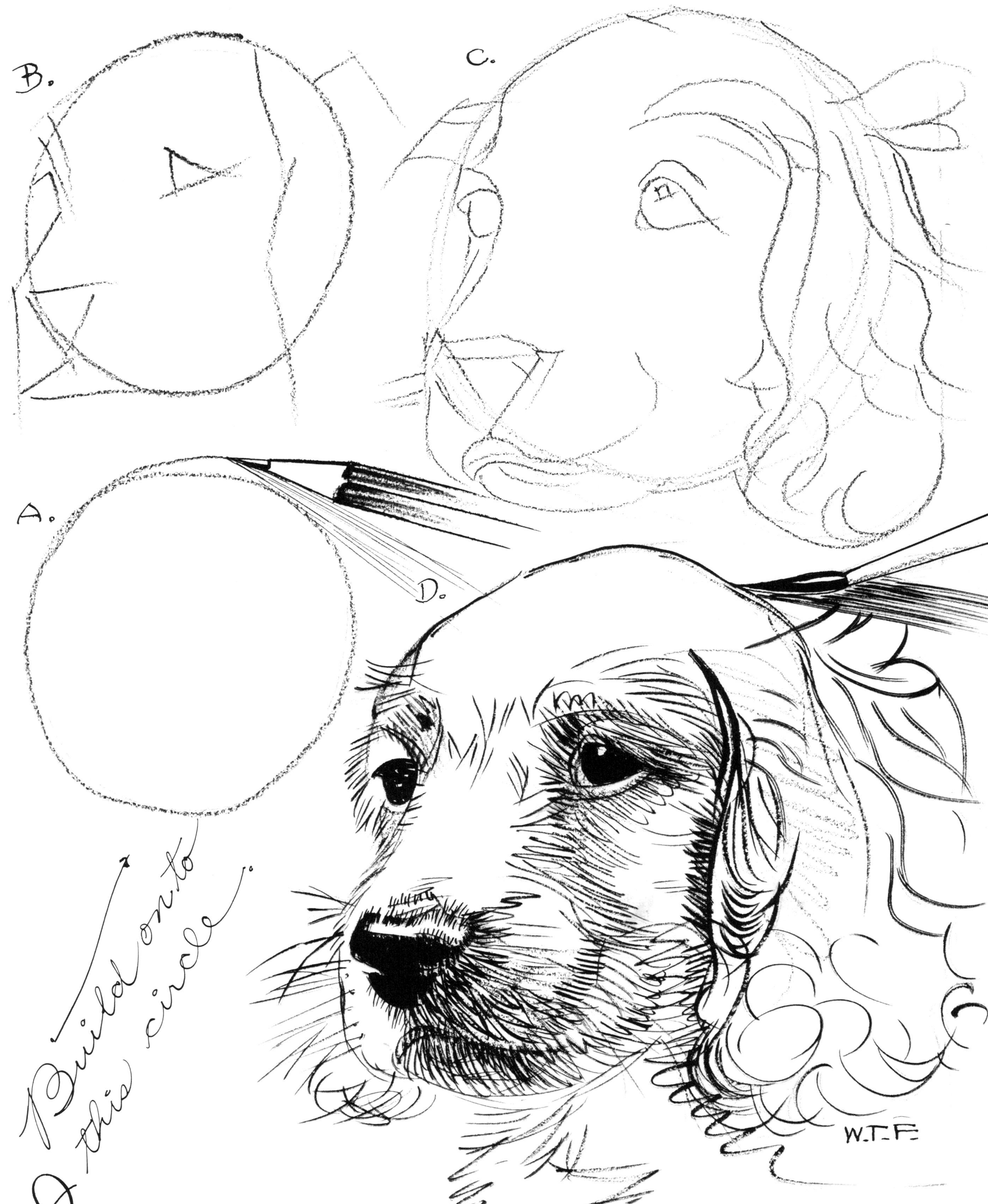

Do not be impatient — just look back on your days when A or Z meant nothing to you and when gradually the printing of CAT, DOG, etc., were great discoveries and began to mean something: then, "My Cat" and "My cat can run" — "My Dog eats meat," etc. Well, we go through the same process in drawing. You learn how to memorize a nose by drawing many of them. That is your A-B-C's, then you learn to place nose, mouth, chin, (like CAT) together. You see, they are a part of your drawing alphabet and when you can draw a head from imagination you must know your drawing alphabet and how to place them together so that they make nice, readable material.

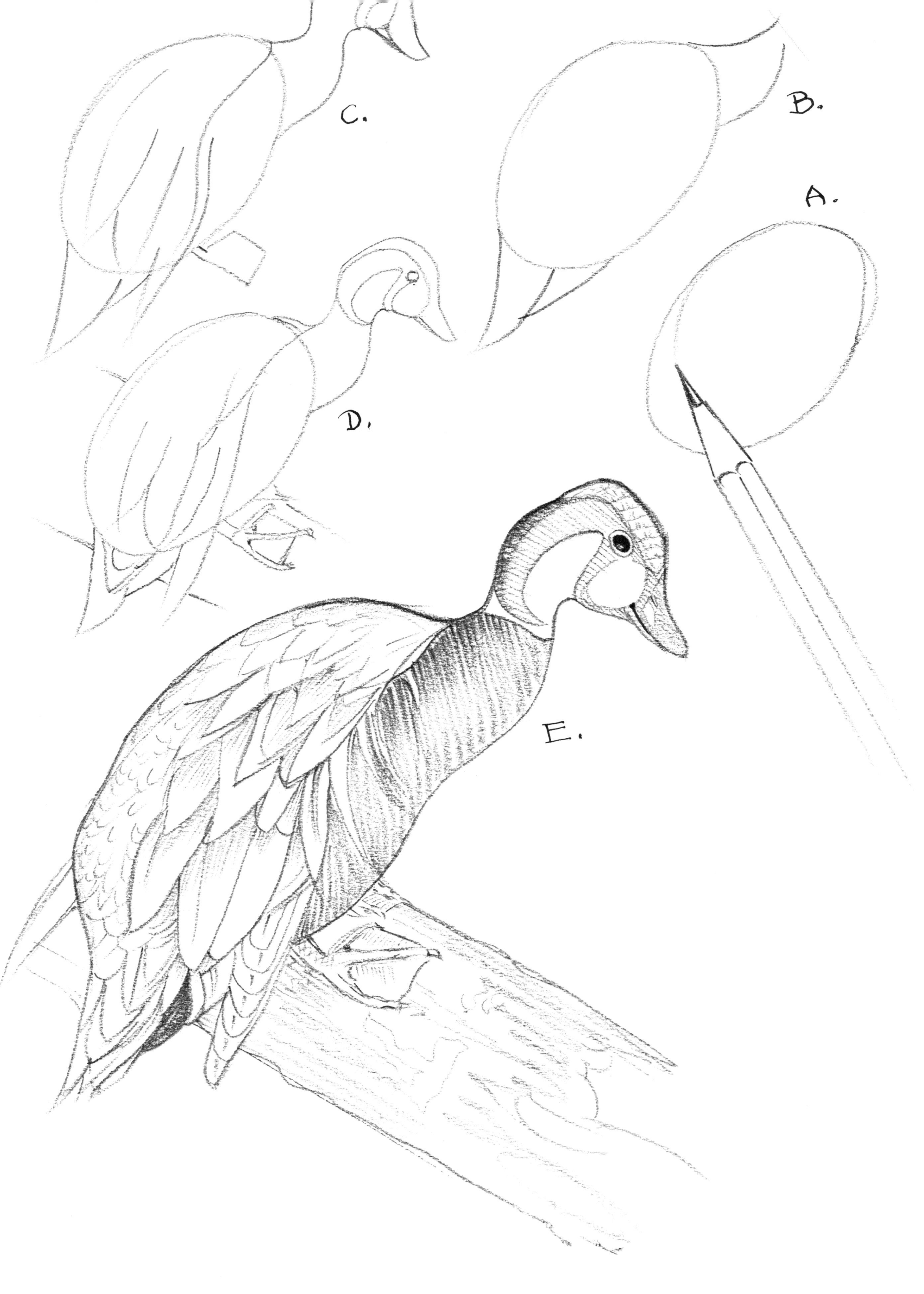
C.
B.
A.
D.
E.

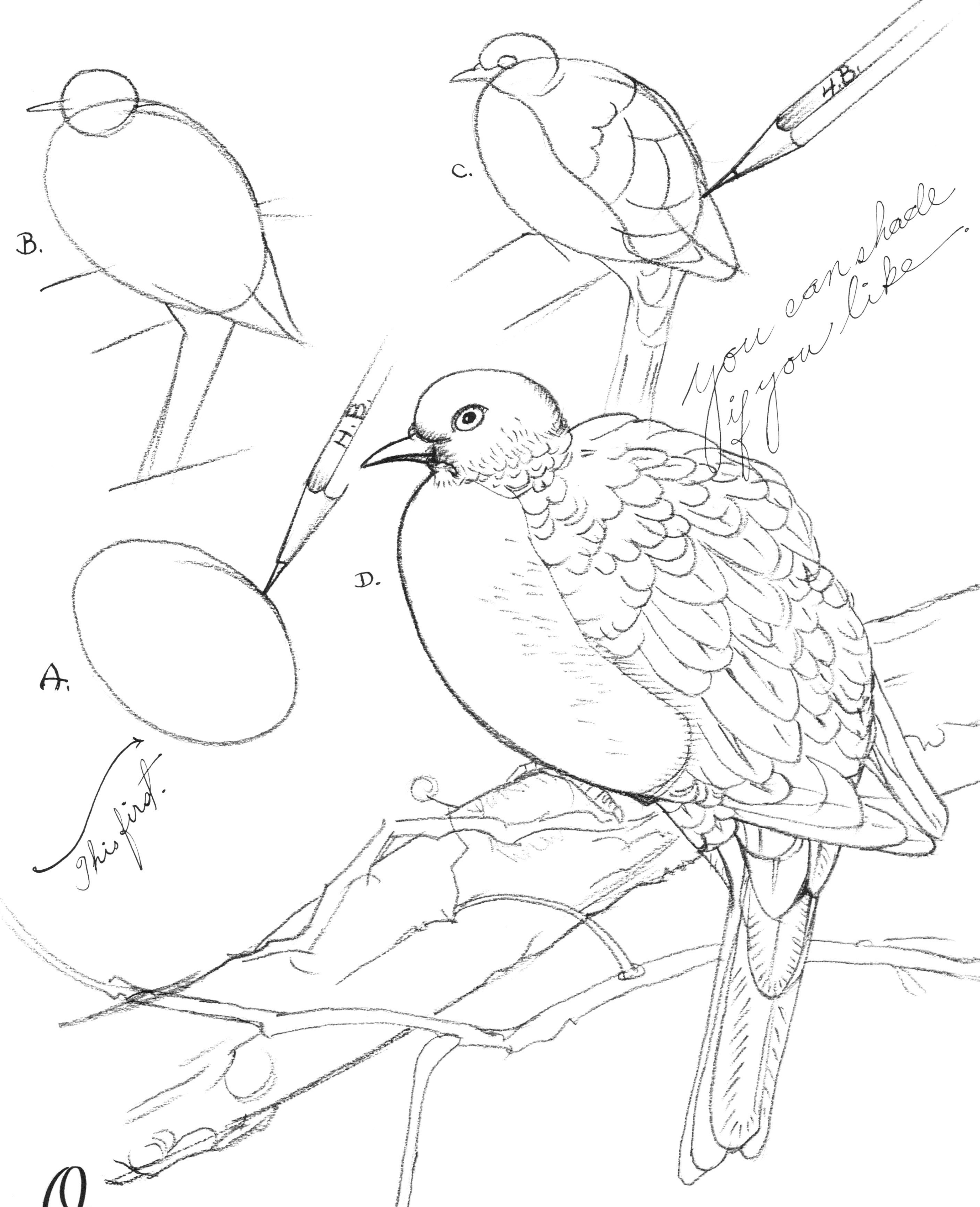

One's mind has a habit at times of wanting to lull one to sleep rather than face a problem that it doesn't want to be bothered with, something the mind does not want to do. Most people's minds are lazy this way, I know mine is, and for your own well-being at times it can and does blank one out, or escape altogether, which is good on things you cannot correct or help. When problems get that way, take a walk. A little time and fresh air does wonders. If you have real problems, face them, never run. You will find your problems right behind and that they can run faster than you. Get rid of them — don't nurse them into big problems. EXCUSE. Shall we Draw?

PARALLEL PERSPECTIVE

LOOKING UP
V.P.
EYE LEVEL
LOOKING DOWN

The principle of Perspective is the same whether used in drawing a book, box or house and is not too difficult to understand. Like mathematics this is only the multiplication table of perspective and when you go beyond this you enter a field as vast and complex as higher mathematics, which is not necessary in drawing but these simple principles are and if you do not know them you will not get very far.

First learn the principles given here and if interested ask to see books on Perspective Drawing listed in back of this book.

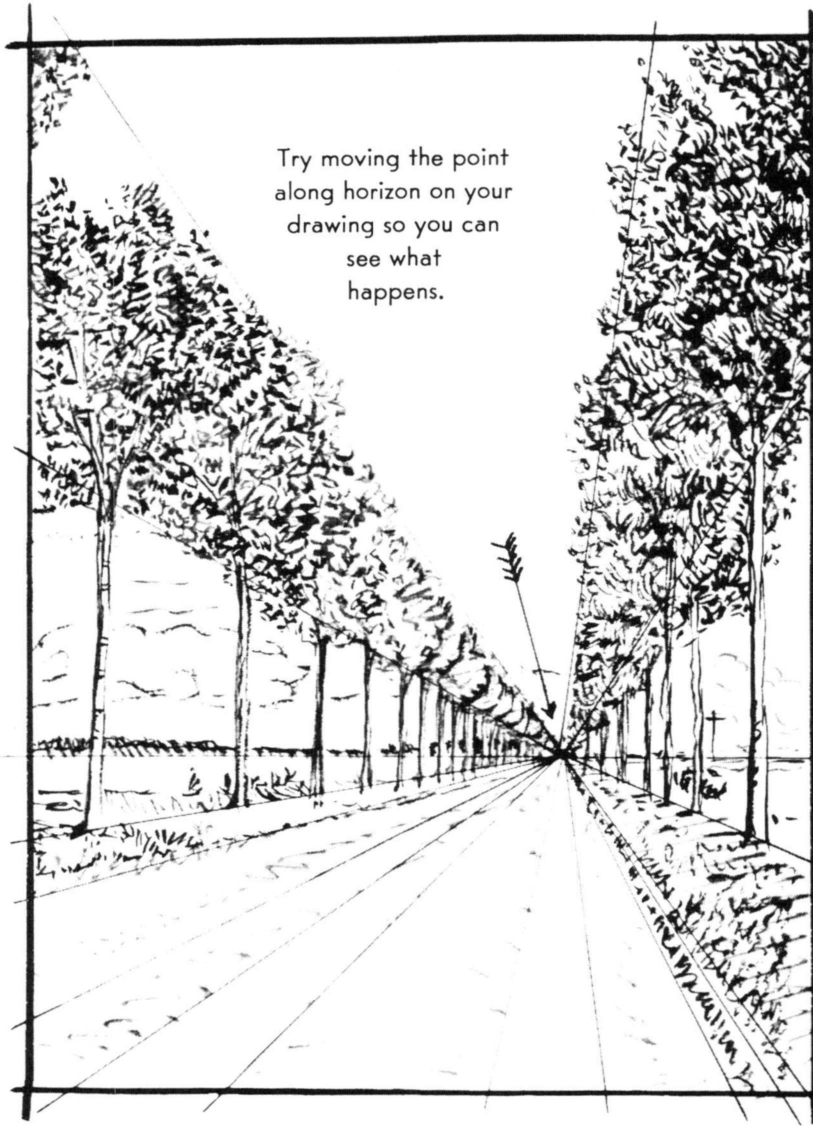

This sketch I made in France is a very good example of parallel or one point perspective. The principle of perspective is the same whether out in the wide open spaces or this could be a hallway in an office building, a street, a room, or the trees could be fence posts or telegraph poles. You have perspective in everything that shows depth, so get acquainted.

V.P. V.P. V.P

When you go beyond this vertical line you begin to see the side of the object.

V.P. Vanishing point
R. Right
L. Left
C. Center

The moment you tip these lines you have two-pointed or Angular Perspective. (See D on next page.)

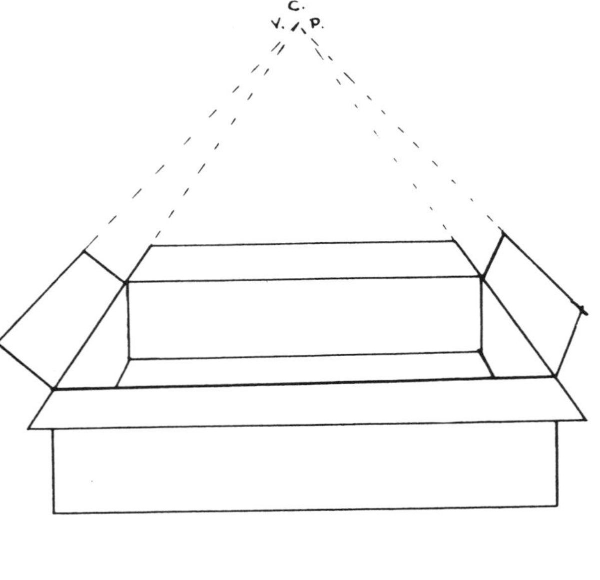

An easy way to grasp the principle of Parallel and Angular Perspective is to draw lines on photographs from magazines, locating the Right and Left vanishing point of buildings, streets, rooms, piano, chairs, tables, etc., or if parallel perspective, the center vanishing point. This will awaken your mind to observe the things around you and be a great help in your art work. First think and draw all the objects in the box. Yes, even a vase.

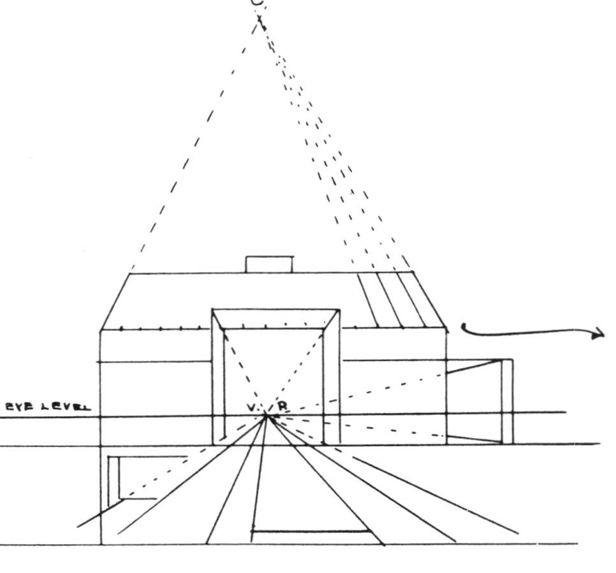

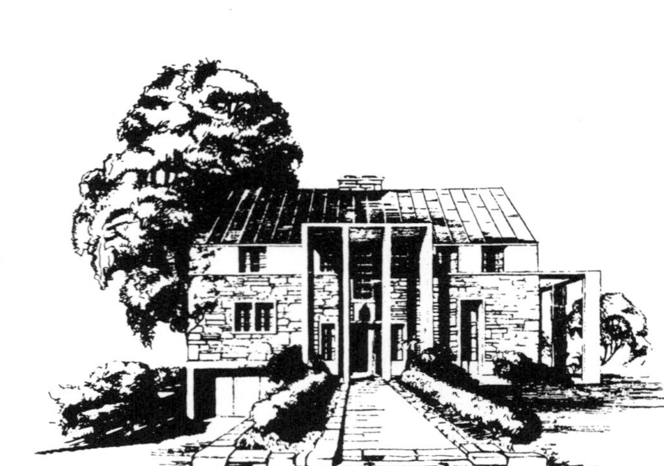

ANGULAR PERSPECTIVE

Why, sure! You use perspective in cartoons. Take time out and go through magazines just looking for drawings; study their perspective.

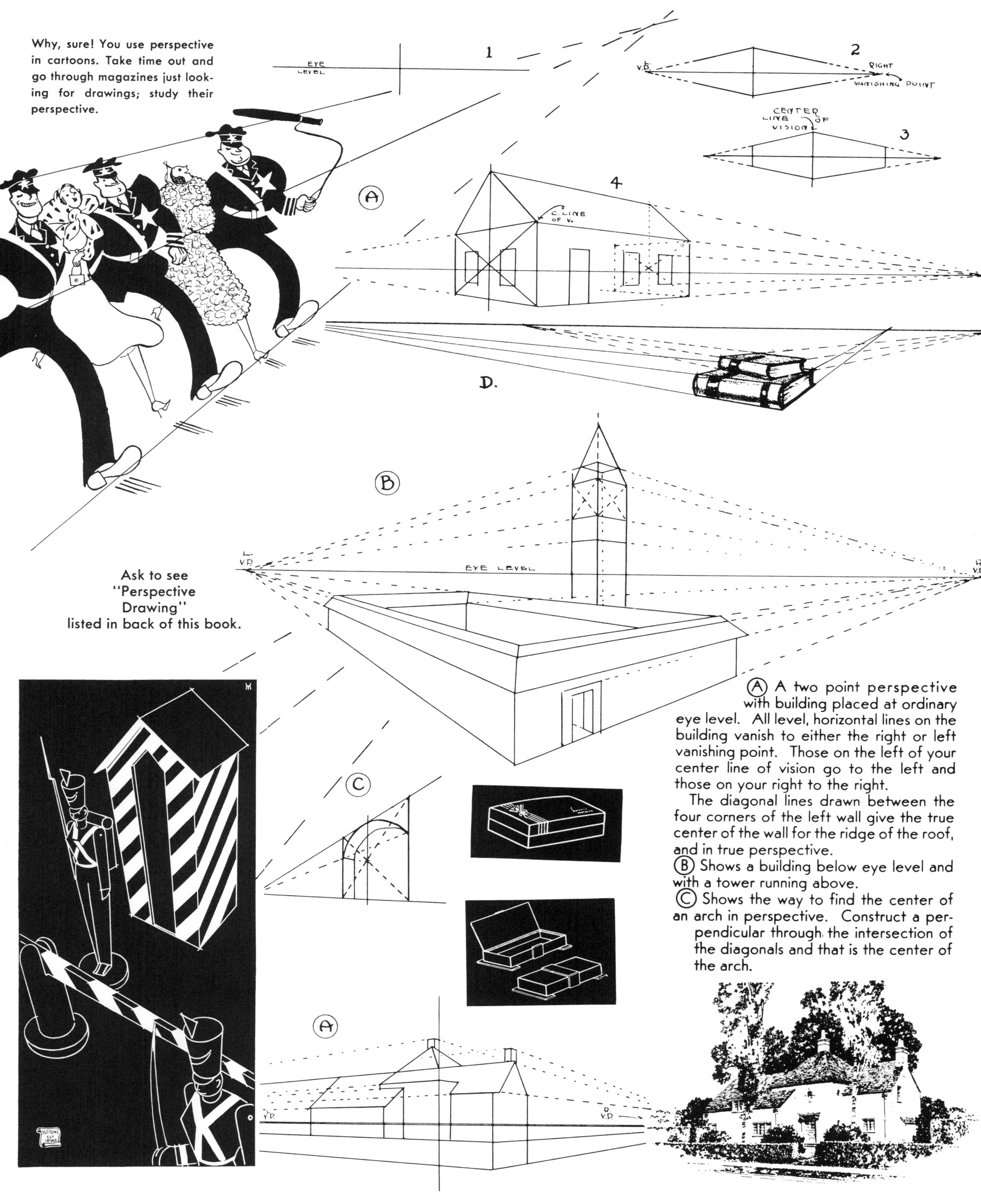

Ask to see "Perspective Drawing" listed in back of this book.

Ⓐ A two point perspective with building placed at ordinary eye level. All level, horizontal lines on the building vanish to either the right or left vanishing point. Those on the left of your center line of vision go to the left and those on your right to the right.

The diagonal lines drawn between the four corners of the left wall give the true center of the wall for the ridge of the roof, and in true perspective.

Ⓑ Shows a building below eye level and with a tower running above.

Ⓒ Shows the way to find the center of an arch in perspective. Construct a perpendicular through the intersection of the diagonals and that is the center of the arch.

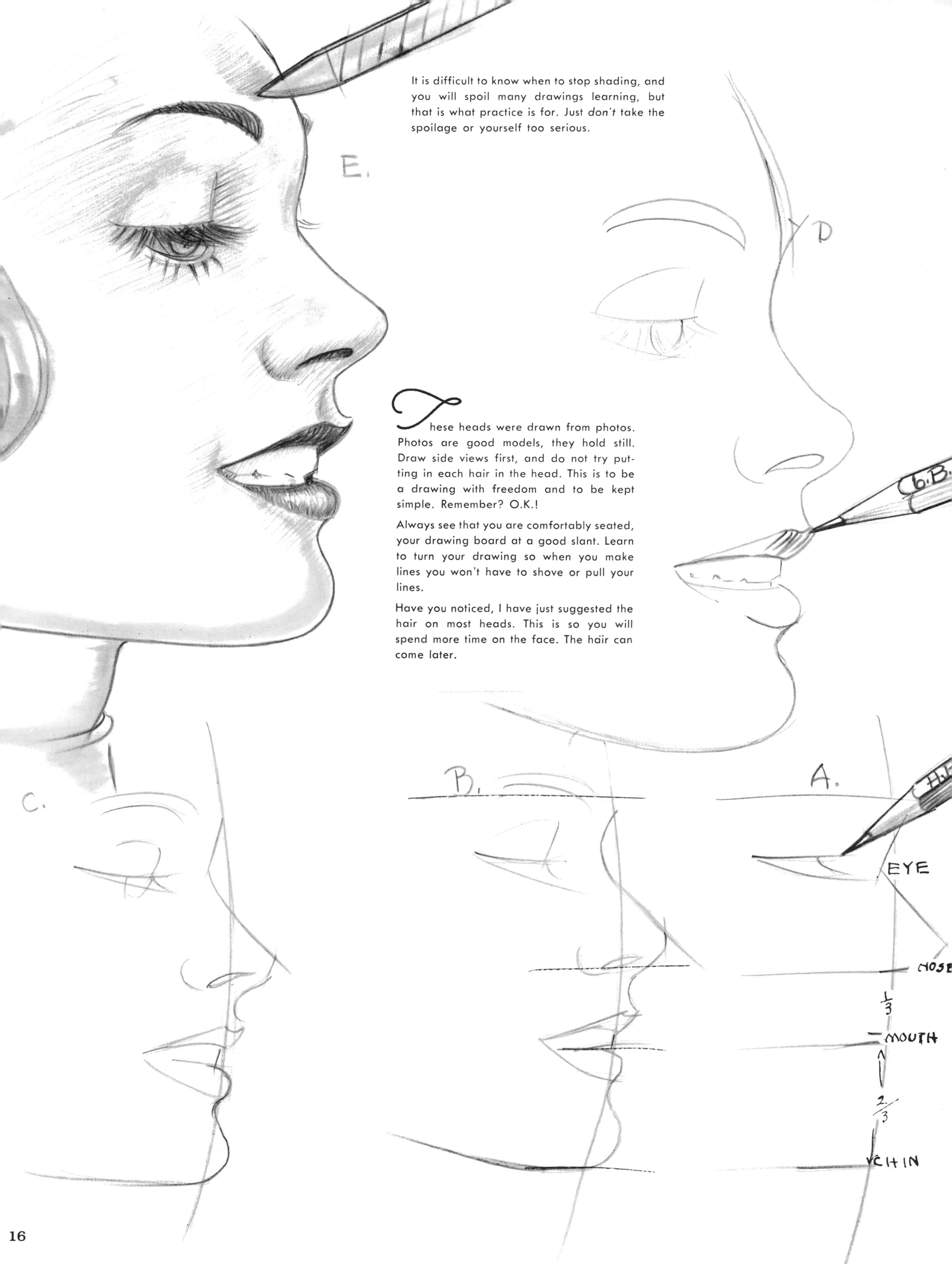

It is difficult to know when to stop shading, and you will spoil many drawings learning, but that is what practice is for. Just *don't* take the spoilage or yourself too serious.

These heads were drawn from photos. Photos are good models, they hold still. Draw side views first, and do not try putting in each hair in the head. This is to be a drawing with freedom and to be kept simple. Remember? O.K.!

Always see that you are comfortably seated, your drawing board at a good slant. Learn to turn your drawing so when you make lines you won't have to shove or pull your lines.

Have you noticed, I have just suggested the hair on most heads. This is so you will spend more time on the face. The hair can come later.

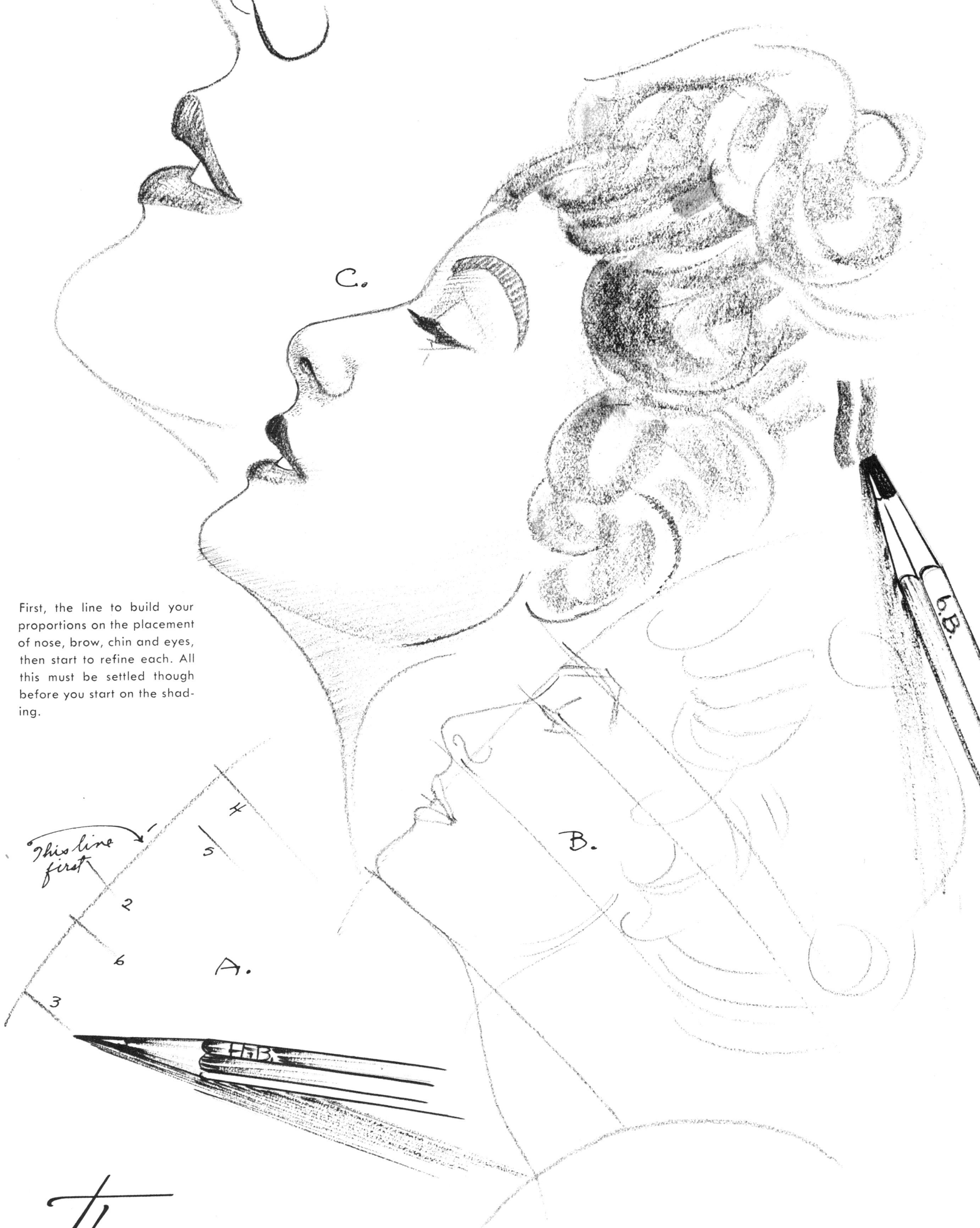

First, the line to build your proportions on the placement of nose, brow, chin and eyes, then start to refine each. All this must be settled though before you start on the shading.

The paper on which you draw can make a vast difference in the looks of your drawings. Here, I have used a cold-pressed paper used for wash drawings, dry brush or pencil and crayon, as I have used. On the opposite page, I have used a smooth bristol board paper, used for pen and ink. Either one you may use finger or stump to blend smooth. To practice, use any paper you have at hand, and the same goes for pencils. Ask to see my book "How to Draw Heads" if you wish to learn more on heads.

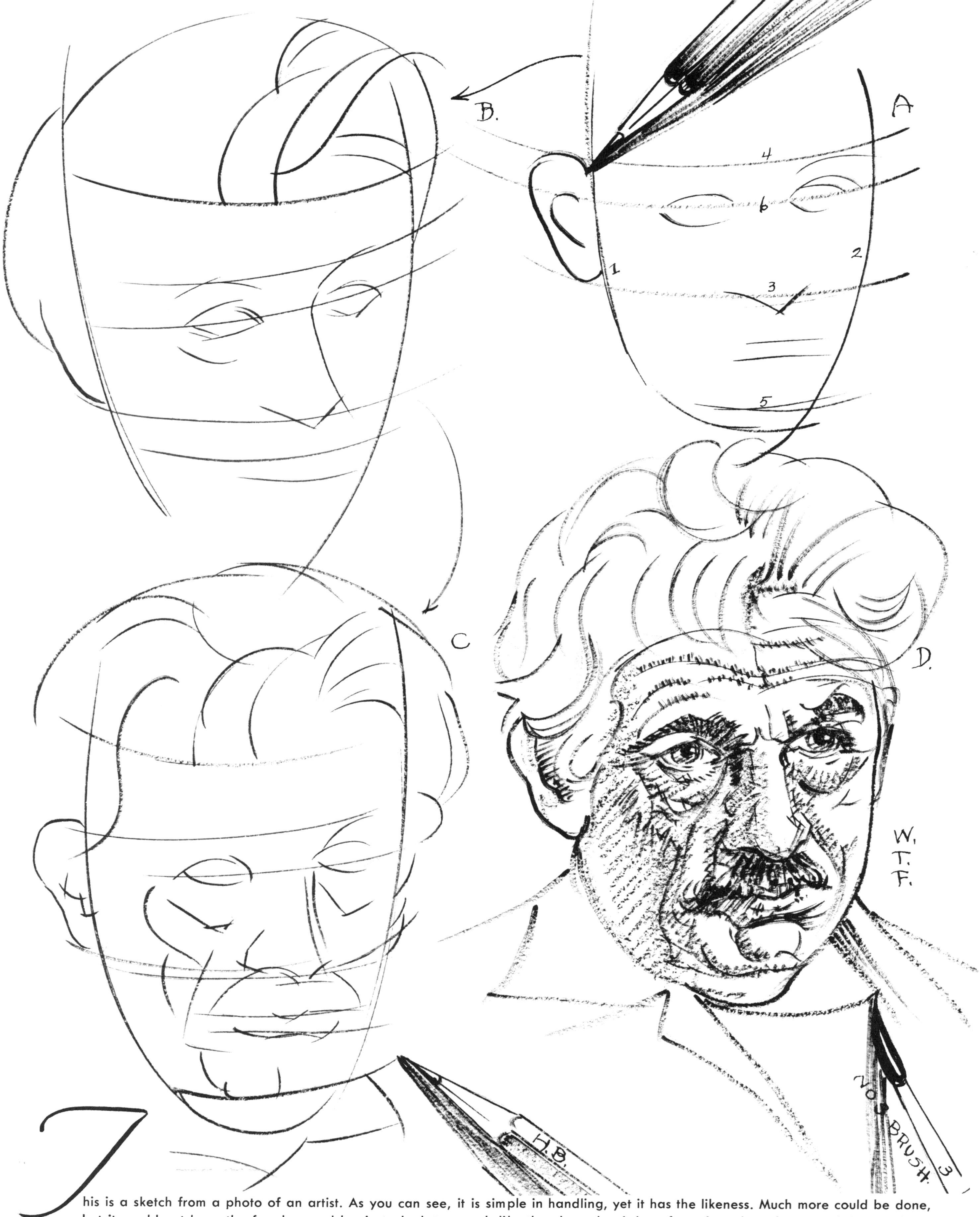

This is a sketch from a photo of an artist. As you can see, it is simple in handling, yet it has the likeness. Much more could be done, but it would not have the freedom and begin to look too much like the photo that I drew from. Learning when to quit is a real art. A brush is a wonderful tool to work with and the Chinese are masters with it.

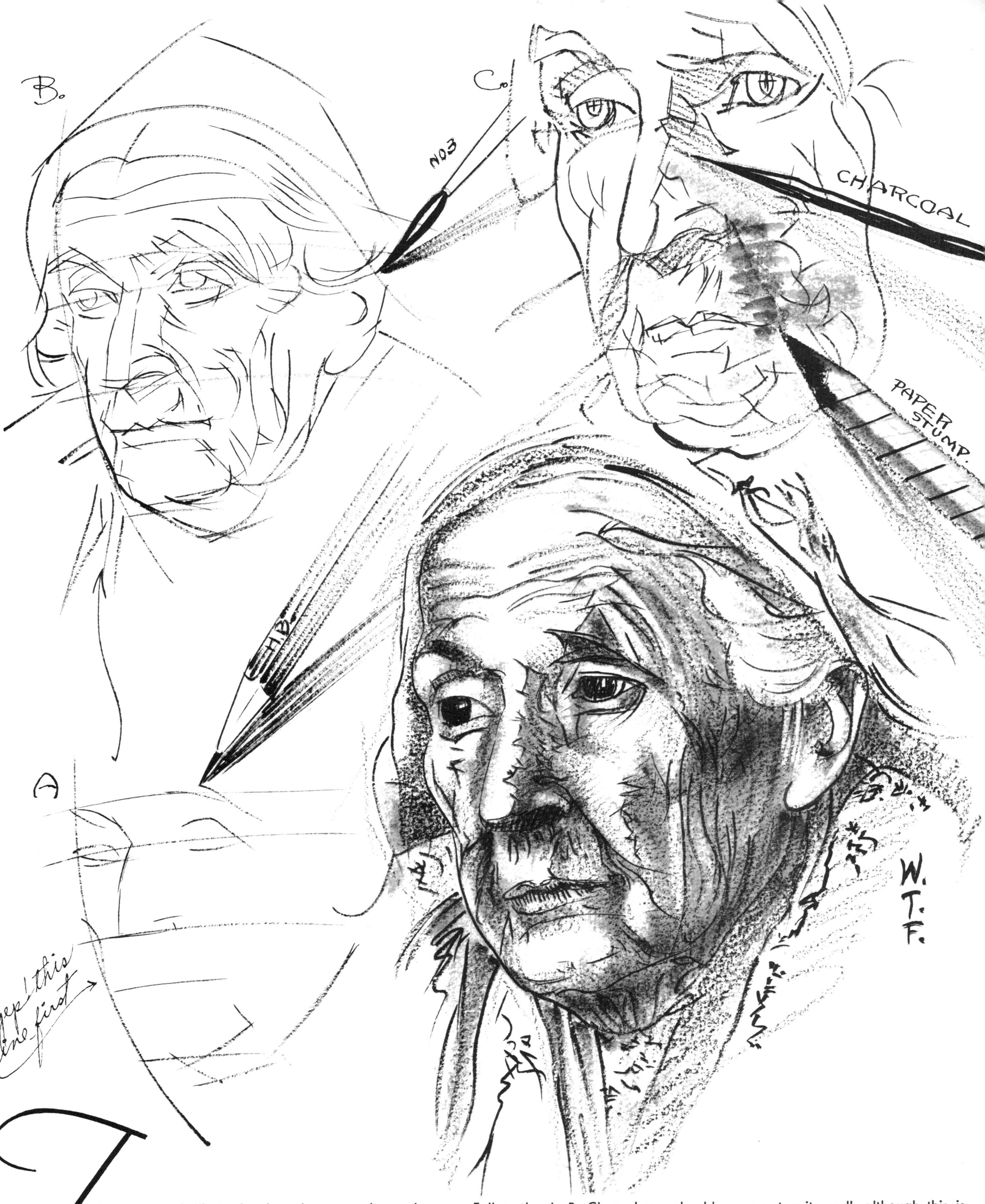

This is on rough illustration board, or use charcoal paper. Follow the A, B, C's and you should come out quite well, although this is not an easy head, but give it a try if you like it. One of the great faults of beginners is the lack of patience he or she has for themselves, expecting their first drawing to be as good as the one someone may have spent years in learning how to do by spoiling many many drawings. Now, don't you be like that, will you.

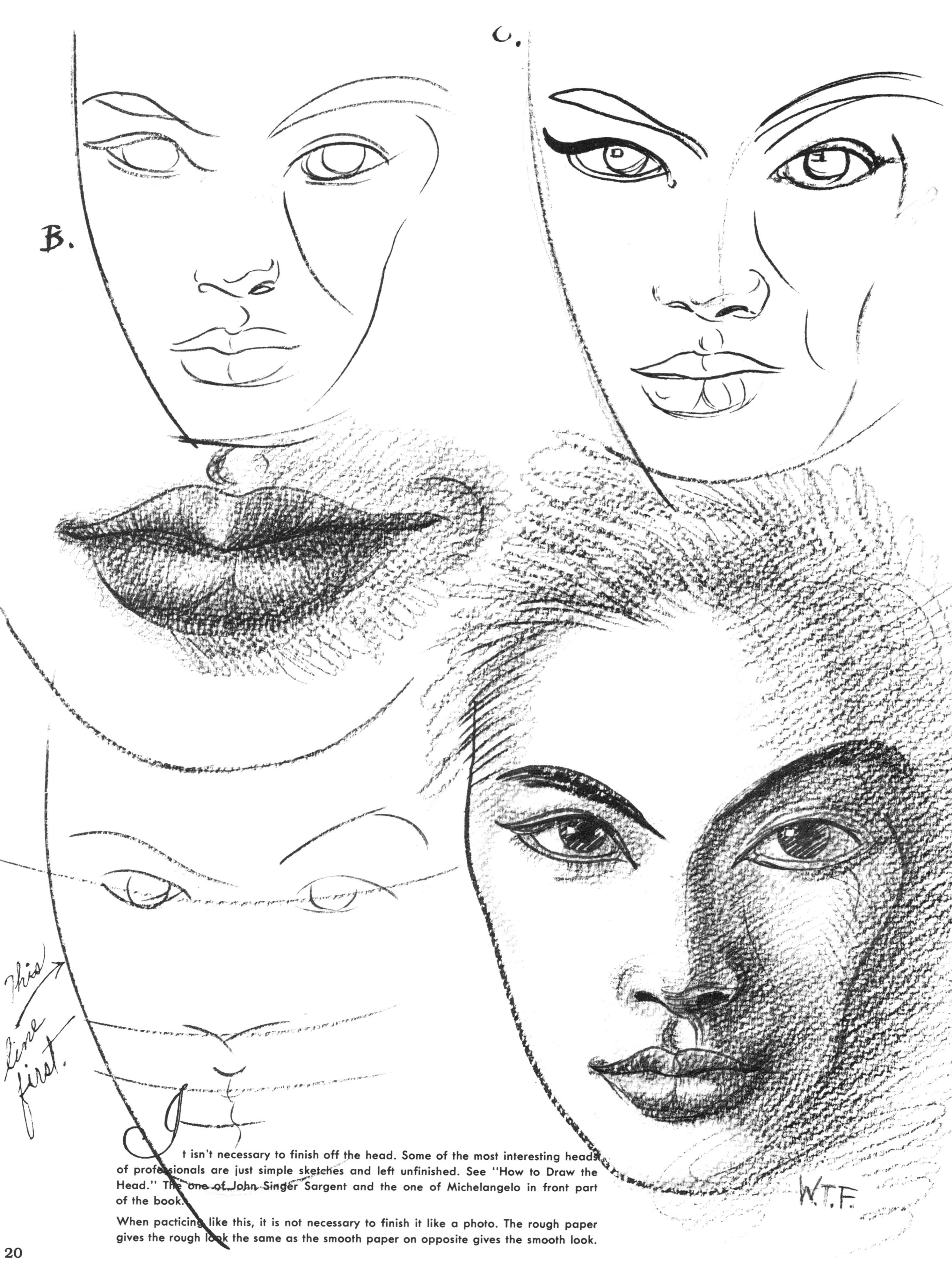

It isn't necessary to finish off the head. Some of the most interesting heads of professionals are just simple sketches and left unfinished. See "How to Draw the Head." The one of John Singer Sargent and the one of Michelangelo in front part of the book.

When pacticing like this, it is not necessary to finish it like a photo. The rough paper gives the rough look the same as the smooth paper on opposite gives the smooth look.

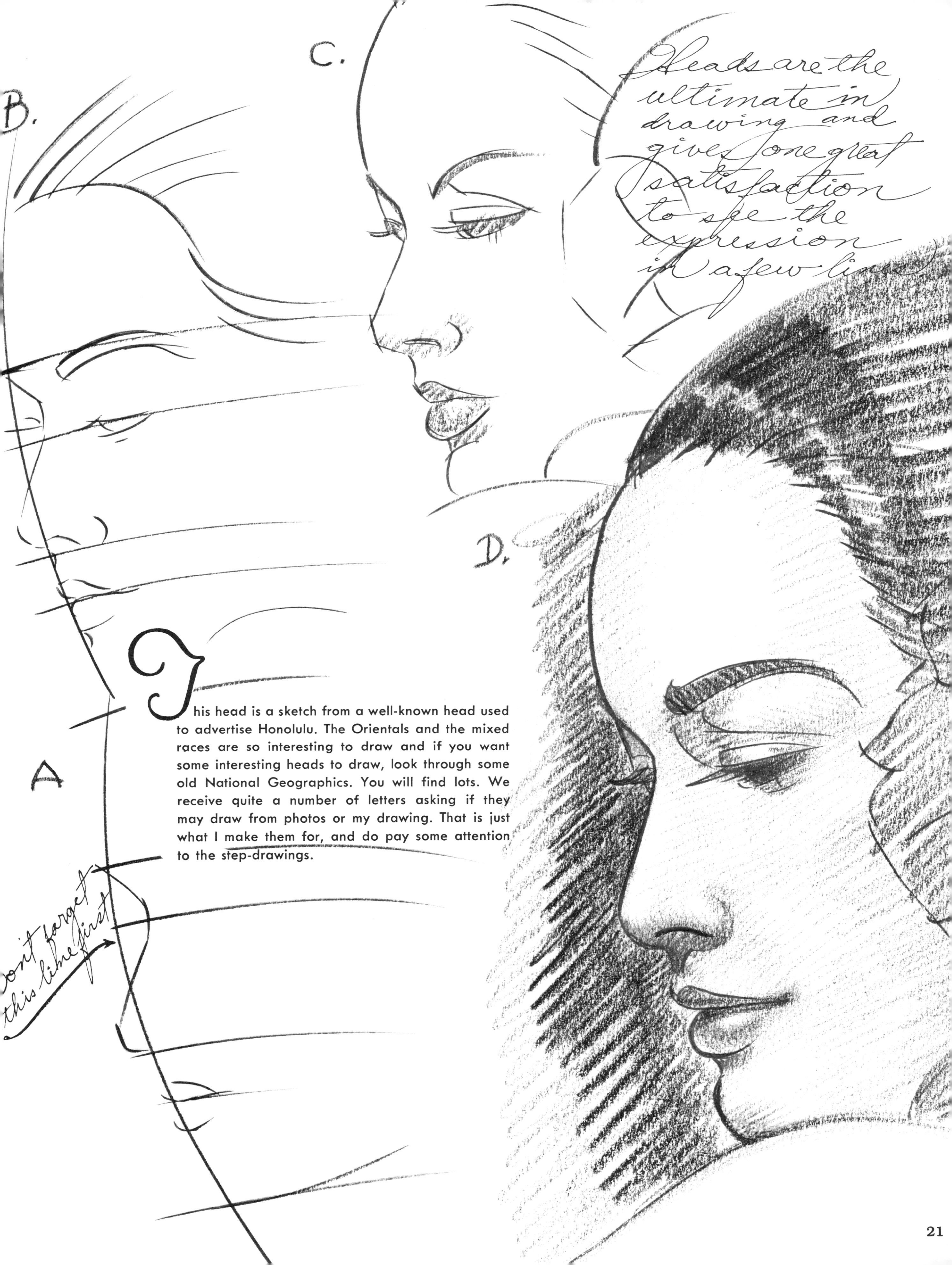

This head is a sketch from a well-known head used to advertise Honolulu. The Orientals and the mixed races are so interesting to draw and if you want some interesting heads to draw, look through some old National Geographics. You will find lots. We receive quite a number of letters asking if they may draw from photos or my drawing. That is just what I make them for, and do pay some attention to the step-drawings.

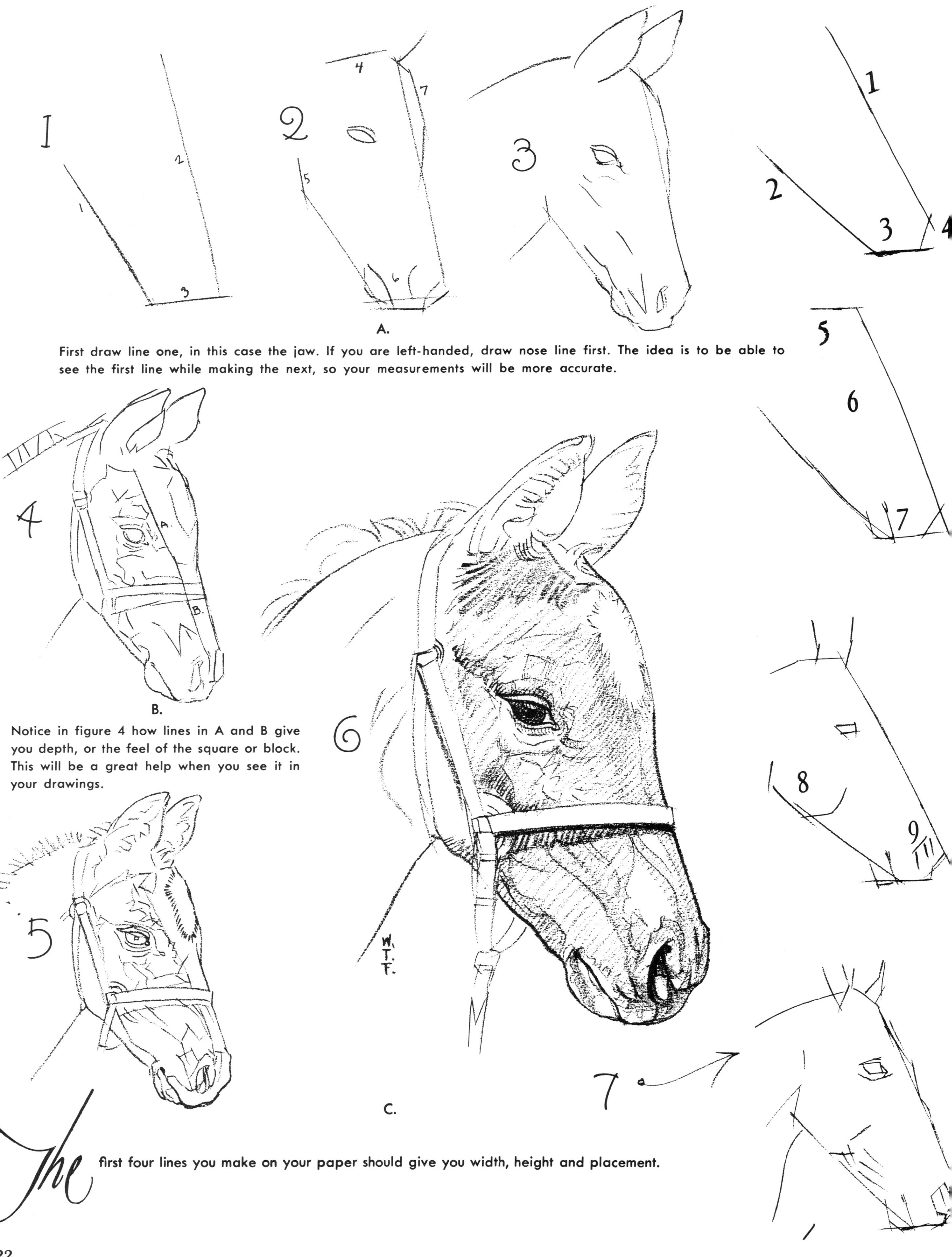

A.

First draw line one, in this case the jaw. If you are left-handed, draw nose line first. The idea is to be able to see the first line while making the next, so your measurements will be more accurate.

B.

Notice in figure 4 how lines in A and B give you depth, or the feel of the square or block. This will be a great help when you see it in your drawings.

C.

The first four lines you make on your paper should give you width, height and placement.

When working from a drawing do not try to follow each brush stroke but let your sense of feel guide you. Sure, you will be confused at first and undecided as to which way the lines should go but your sense of direction will become sharper through mistakes and trying. All artists must go through this — it is the part of learning. Just remember the one who never makes a mistake has never tried or he is kidding himself.

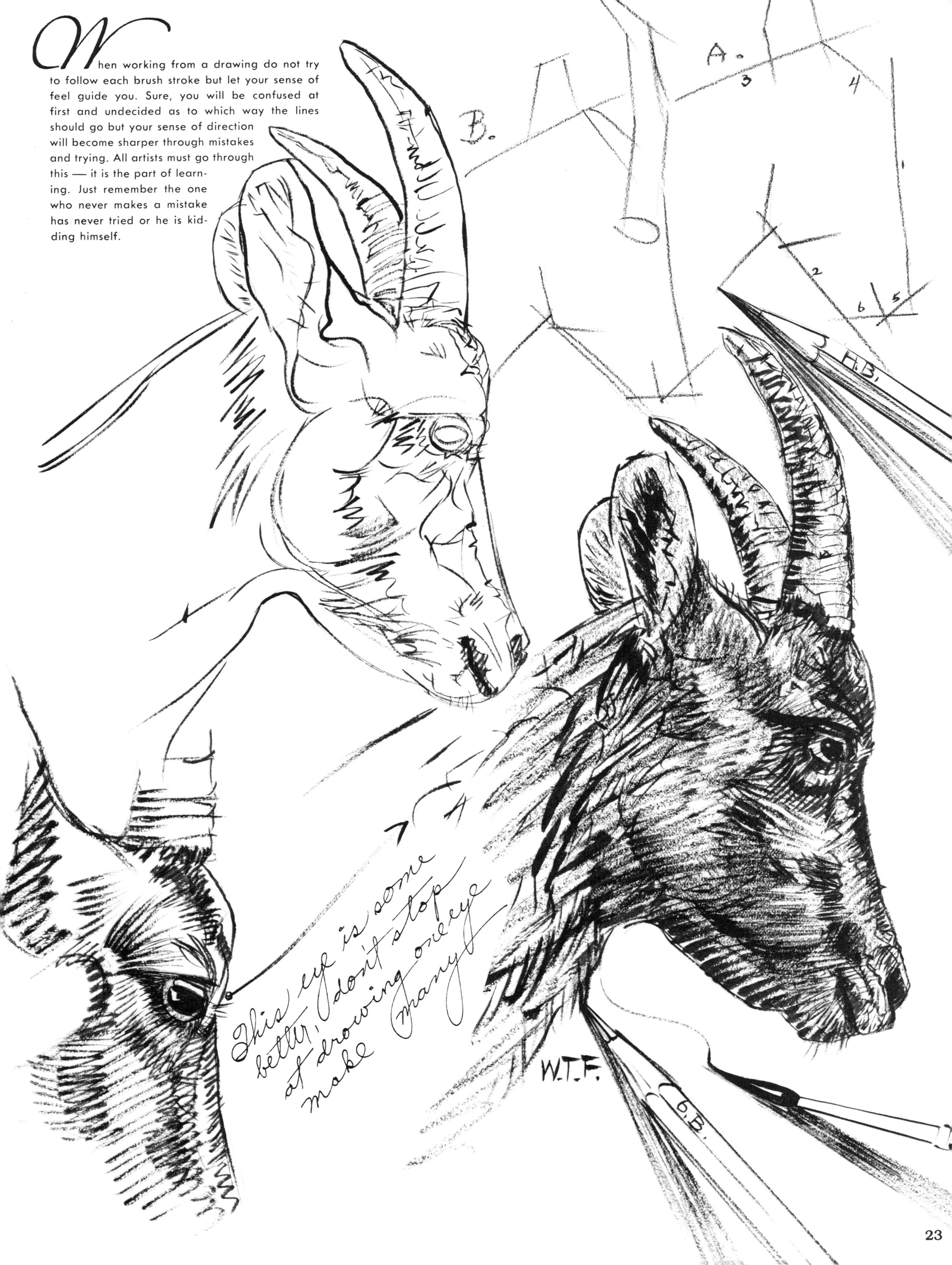

The ABC's of Initials

GOOD LETTERING IS NOT EASY IT TAKES MUCH PRACTICE BUT TRY IT ~~~ LETTERING IS PART OF DRAWING

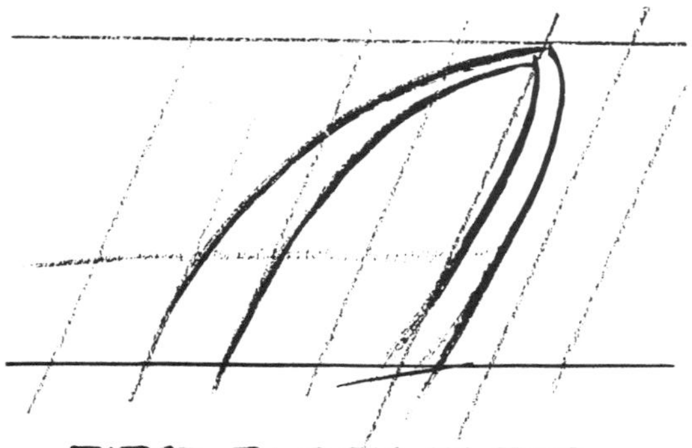

FIRST BLOCK IN FOR PLACEMENT

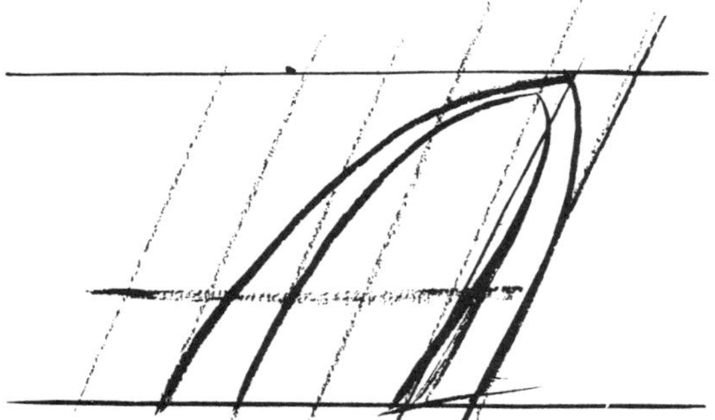

ROUND OUT THE LETTER AND CORRECT PROPORTIONS

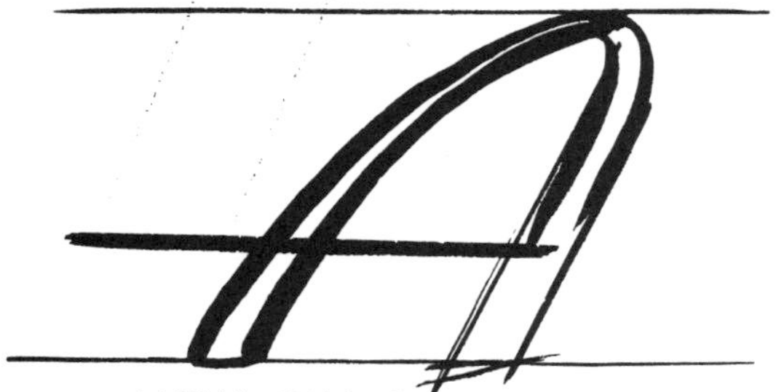

NOW INK IN WITH BRUSH AND PEN

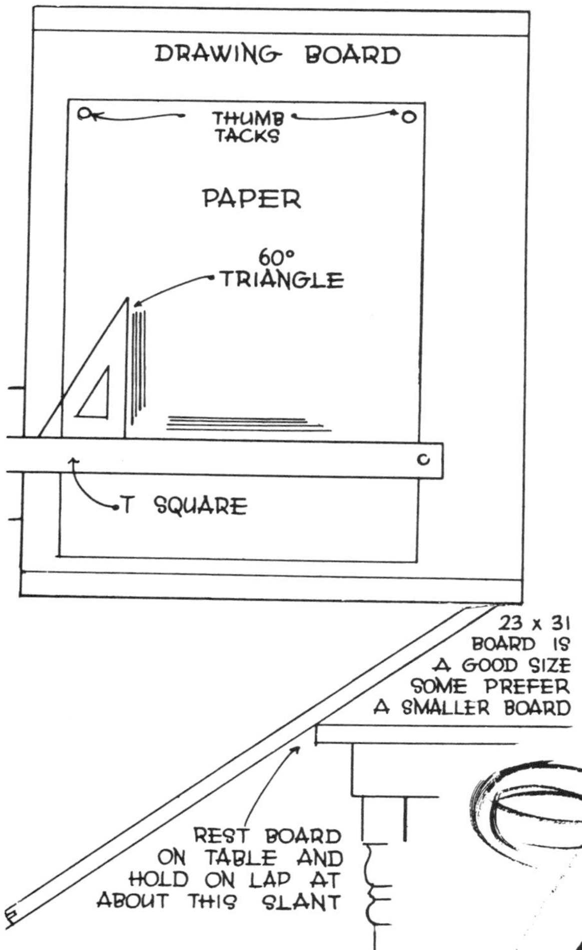
DRAWING BOARD
THUMB TACKS
PAPER
60° TRIANGLE
T SQUARE
23 x 31 BOARD IS A GOOD SIZE SOME PREFER A SMALLER BOARD
REST BOARD ON TABLE AND HOLD ON LAP AT ABOUT THIS SLANT

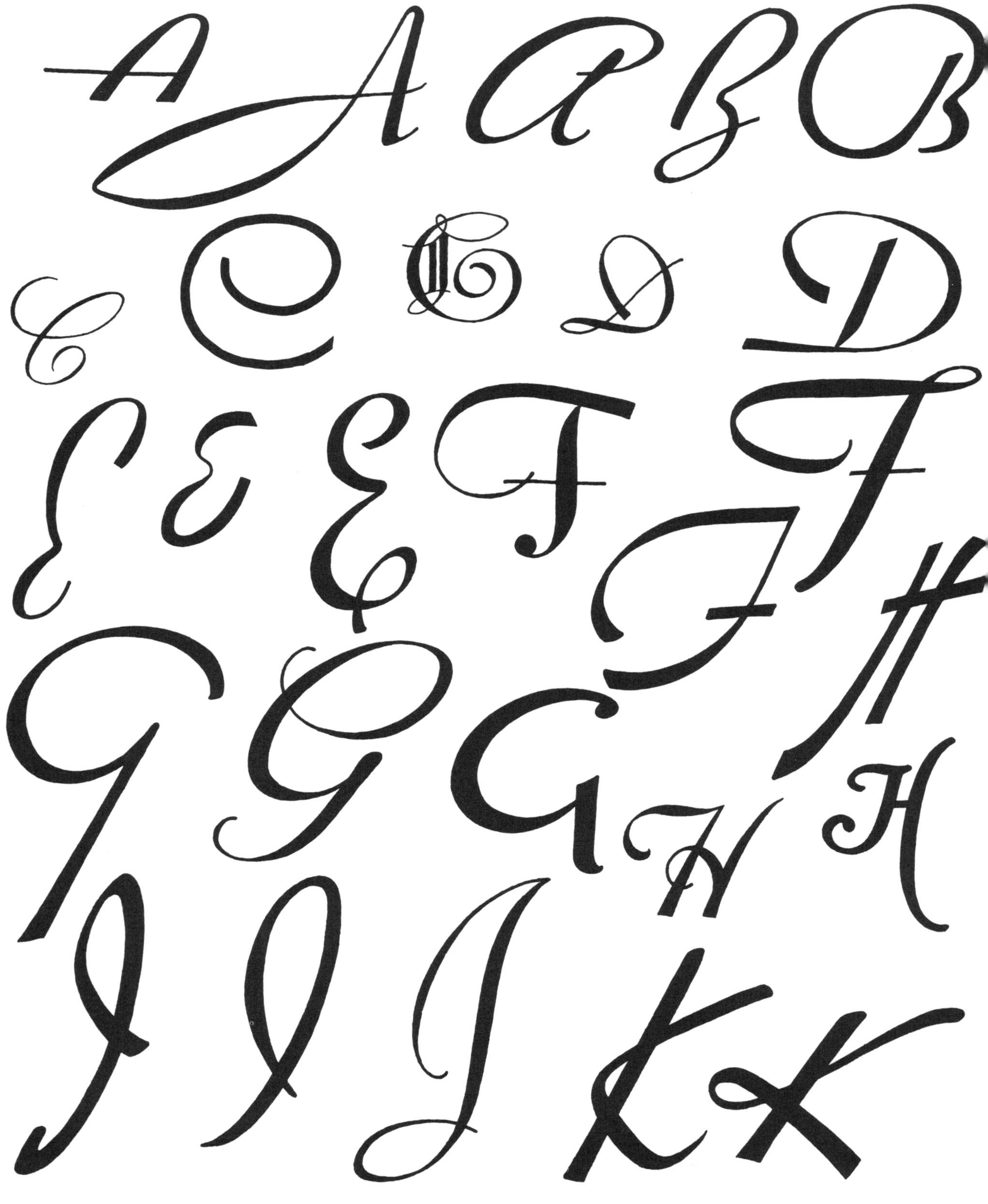

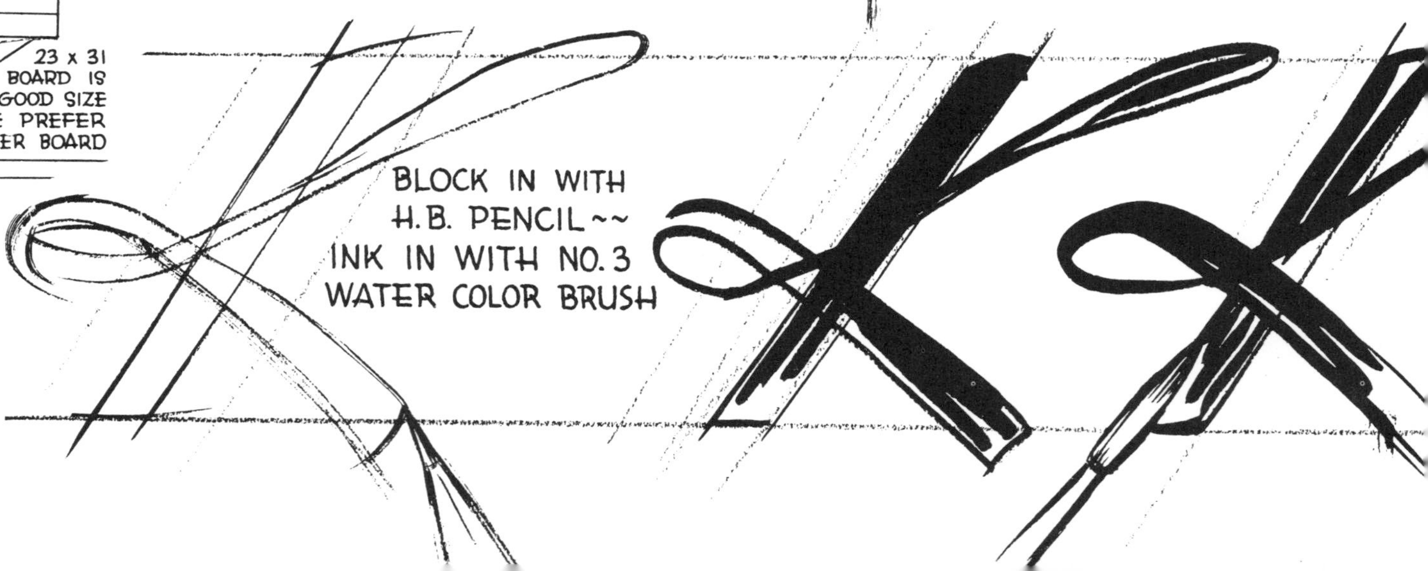

BLOCK IN WITH H.B. PENCIL~~ INK IN WITH NO. 3 WATER COLOR BRUSH

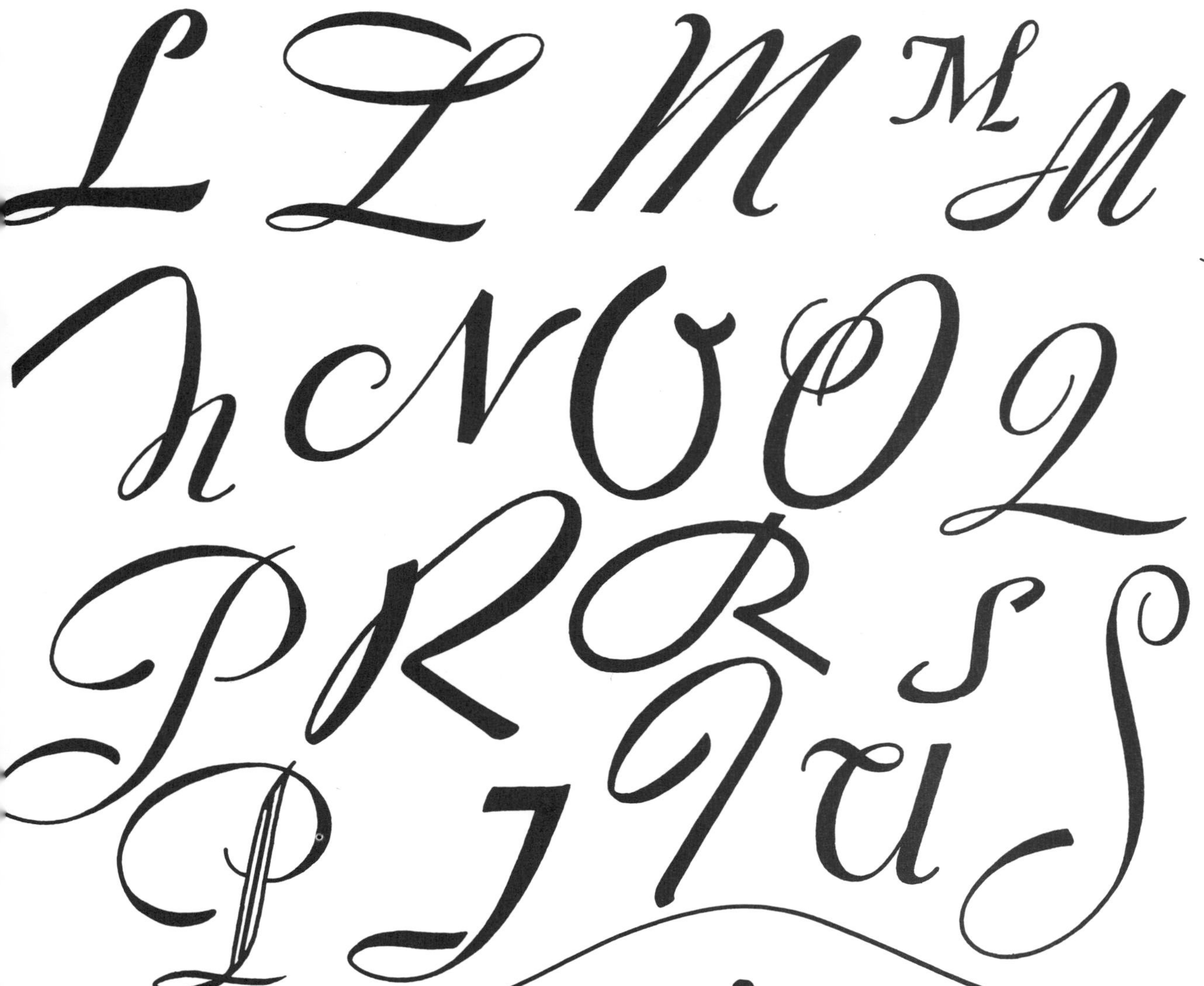

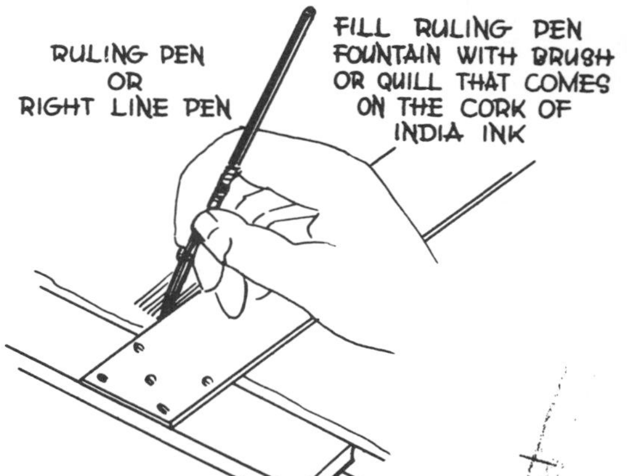
RULING PEN
OR
RIGHT LINE PEN
FILL RULING PEN
FOUNTAIN WITH BRUSH
OR QUILL THAT COMES
ON THE CORK OF
INDIA INK

INK IN WITH RULING PEN WHERE YOU HAVE STRAIGHT LINES ~~~~~

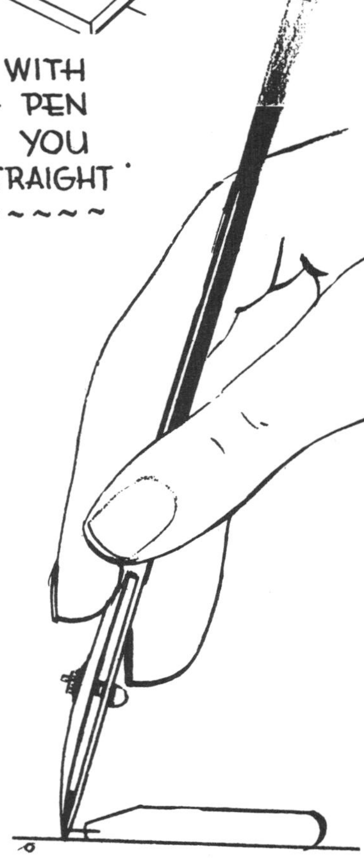

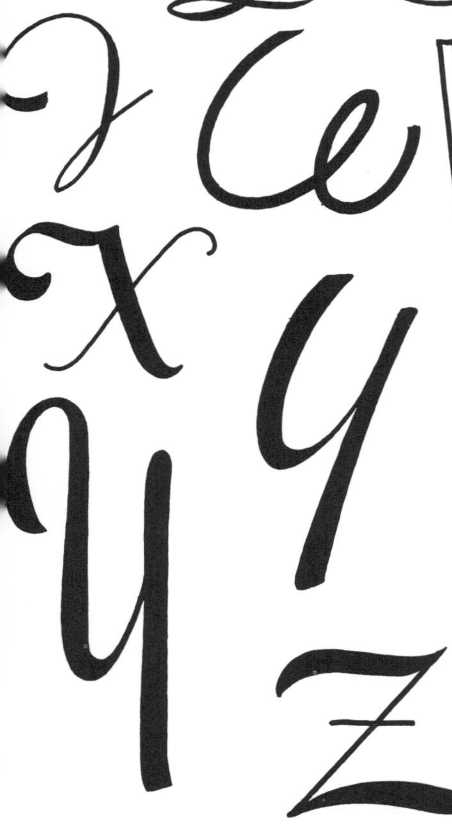

INITIAL LETTERS OR CAPITALS ARE USED TO GOOD ADVANTAGE IN ADDING INTEREST AND INDIVIDUALITY TO TYPE OR HAND LETTERING. DO NOT WAIT UNTIL YOU HAVE A CAPITAL TO MAKE BEFORE PRACTICING, IT TAKES MUCH PRACTICE TO GAIN FREEDOM.

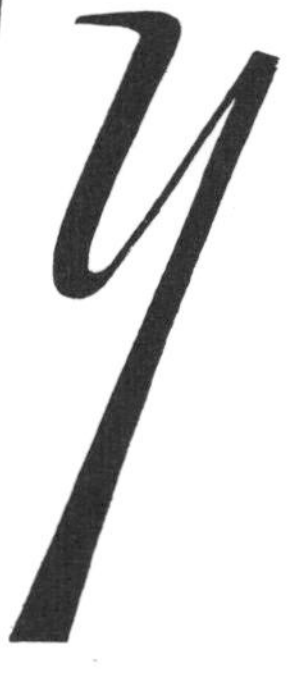

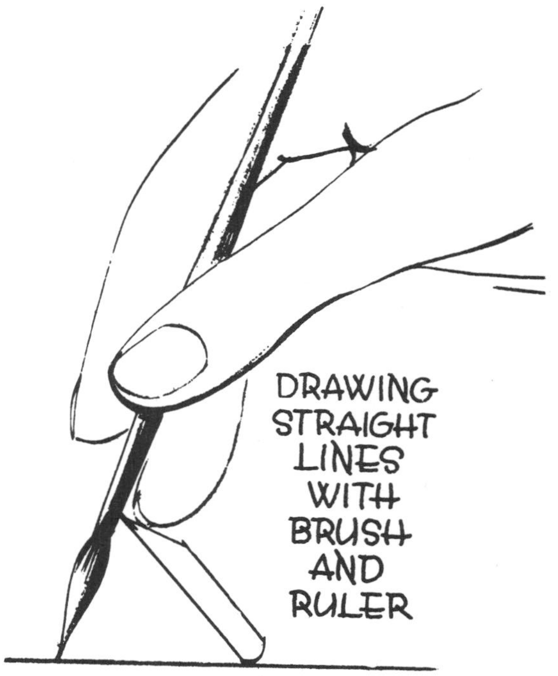

DRAWING STRAIGHT LINES WITH BRUSH AND RULER

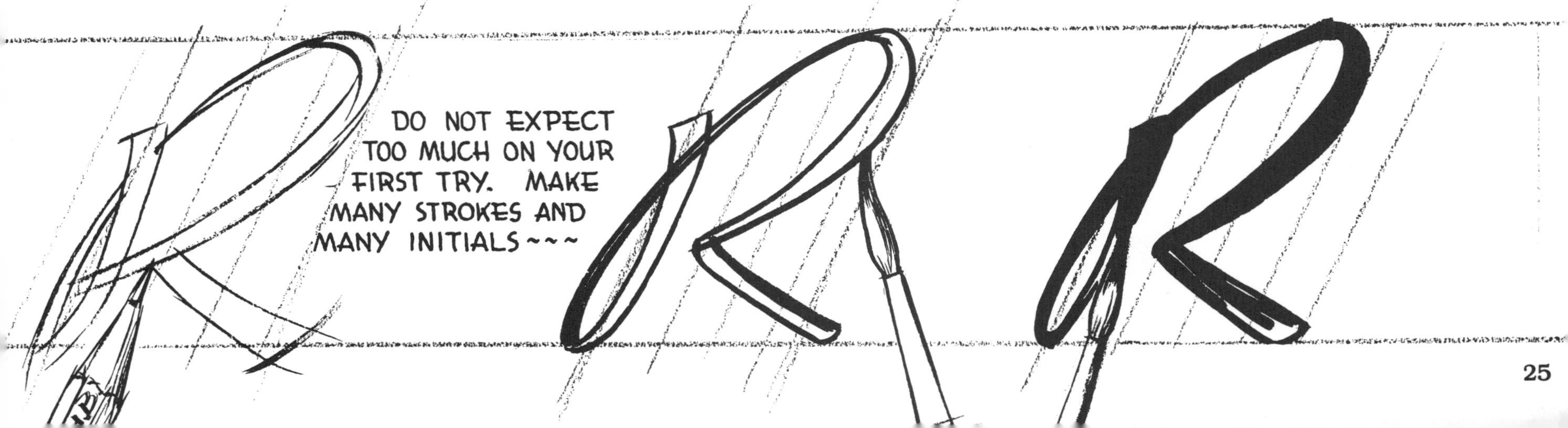
DO NOT EXPECT
TOO MUCH ON YOUR
FIRST TRY. MAKE
MANY STROKES AND
MANY INITIALS ~~~

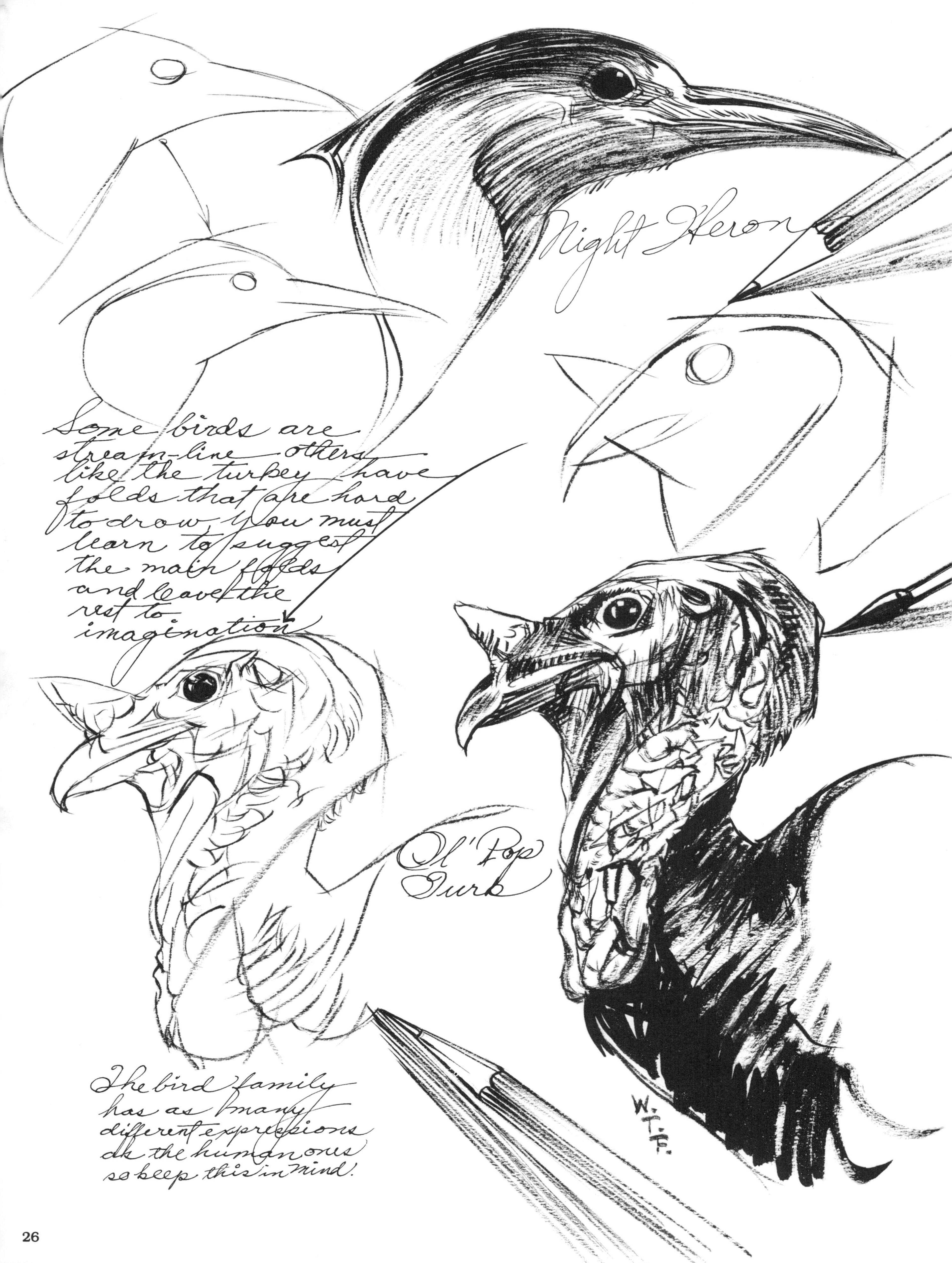
Night Heron
Some birds are
stream-line others
like the turkey have
folds that are hard
to draw. You must
learn to suggest
the main folds
and leave the
rest to
imagination
Ol' Pop
Turk
The bird family
has as many
different expressions
as the human ones
so keep this in mind.
W.T.F.

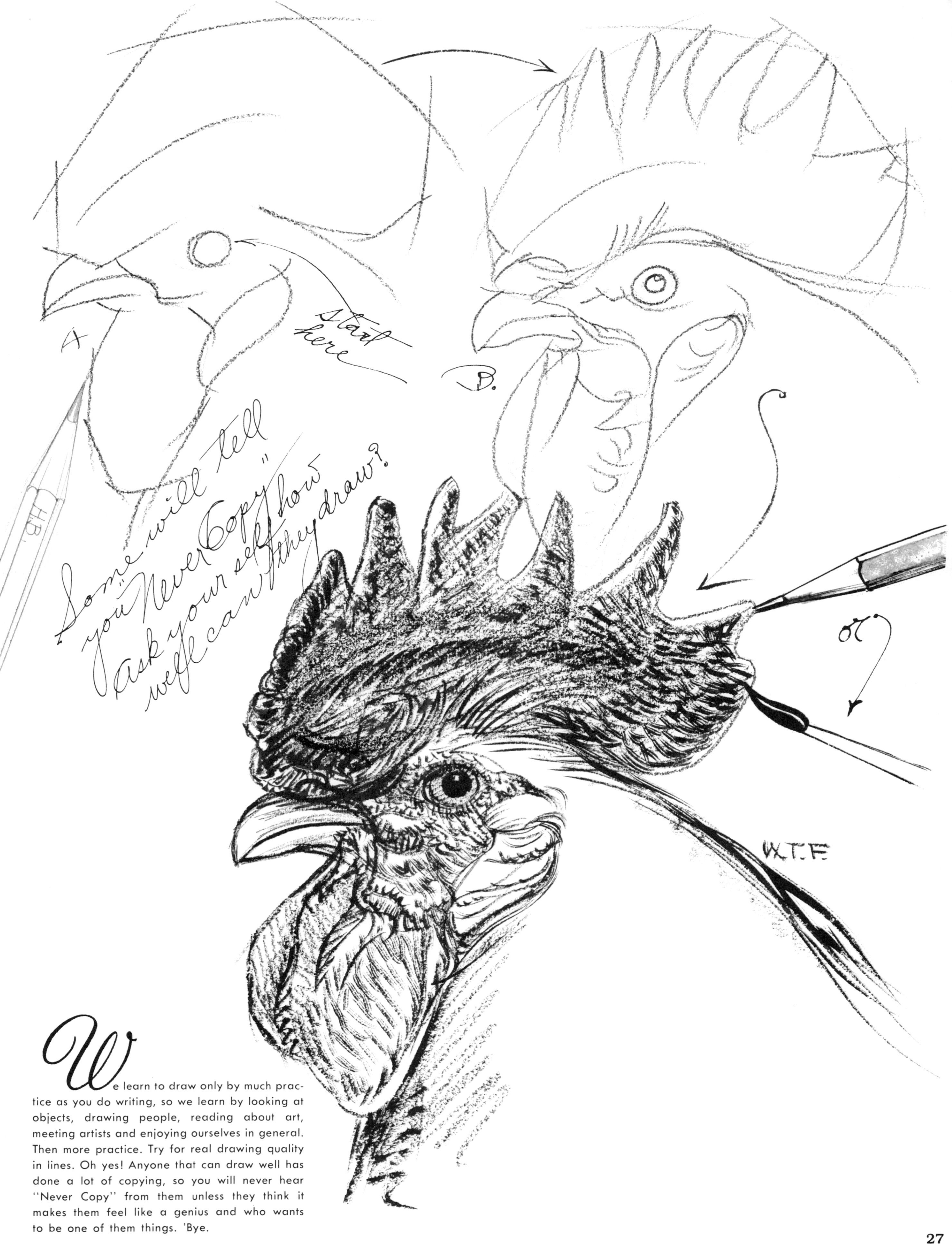

We learn to draw only by much practice as you do writing, so we learn by looking at objects, drawing people, reading about art, meeting artists and enjoying ourselves in general. Then more practice. Try for real drawing quality in lines. Oh yes! Anyone that can draw well has done a lot of copying, so you will never hear "Never Copy" from them unless they think it makes them feel like a genius and who wants to be one of them things. 'Bye.

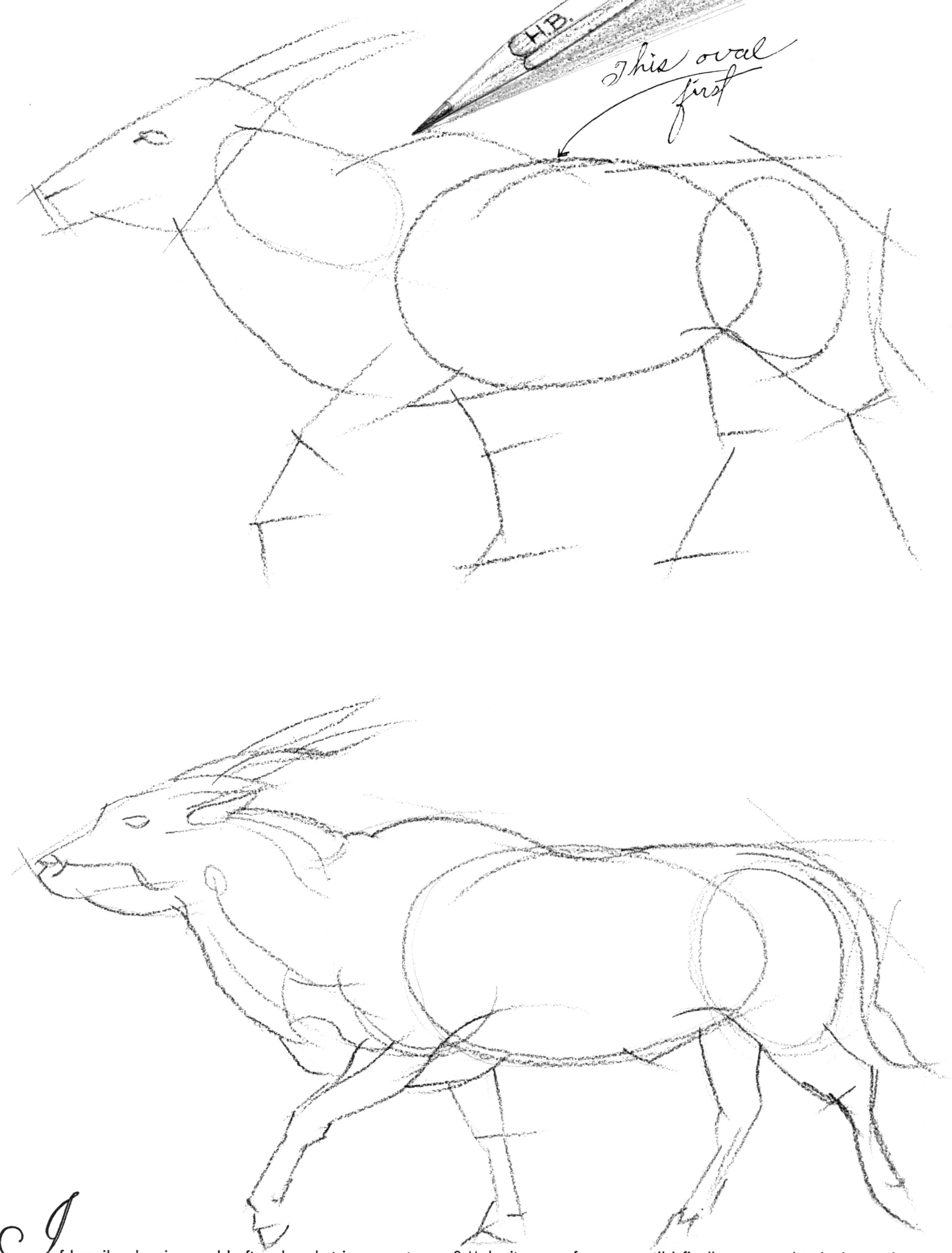

If I spoil a drawing, and I often do, what is my next move? Make it over, of course, until I finally get one that looks good. The easy way would be to just forget it, but I wouldn't have learned and that may be another stumbling block whenever I started another drawing that was similar. Sure, I could say "I am much better at drawing apples," but who wants to draw apples all his life. Do I make myself clear? Any problem in life is so much easier to face if decided right away. Problems are like debts, they are a nuisance when not taken care of.

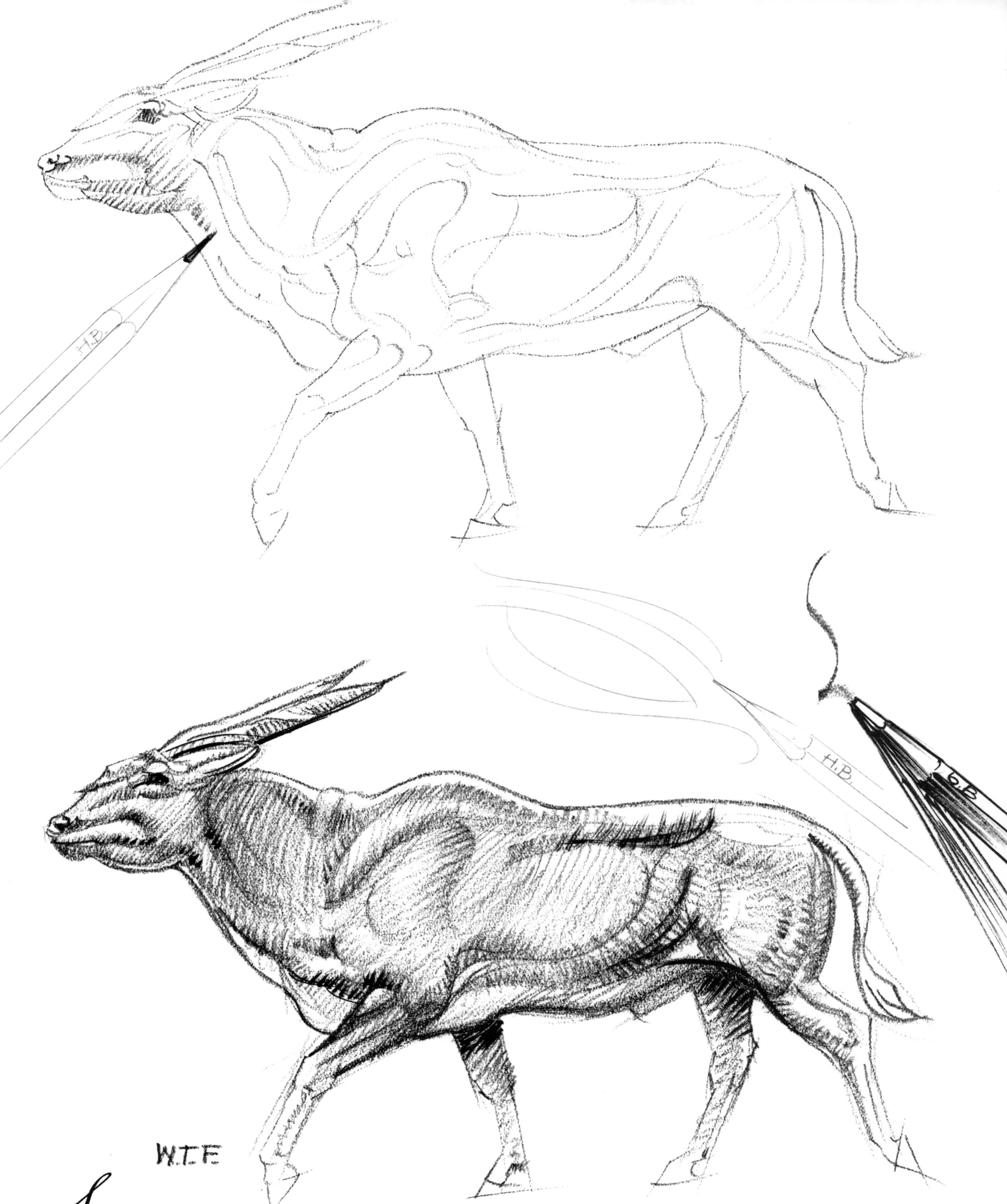

So often a drawing may look easy to do, but when you get into it, it may not be so easy. This, I found with Dr. Clark's African Eland. It is from one of his beautiful bas-reliefs. Shall we start on the drawing? Start shading on the head. Do not finish, but work toward the back and do your shading like you were putting several coats of paint on a house, one coat over the other. I cannot repeat too often, unless you have a good blocking-in, the shading will not improve your picture.

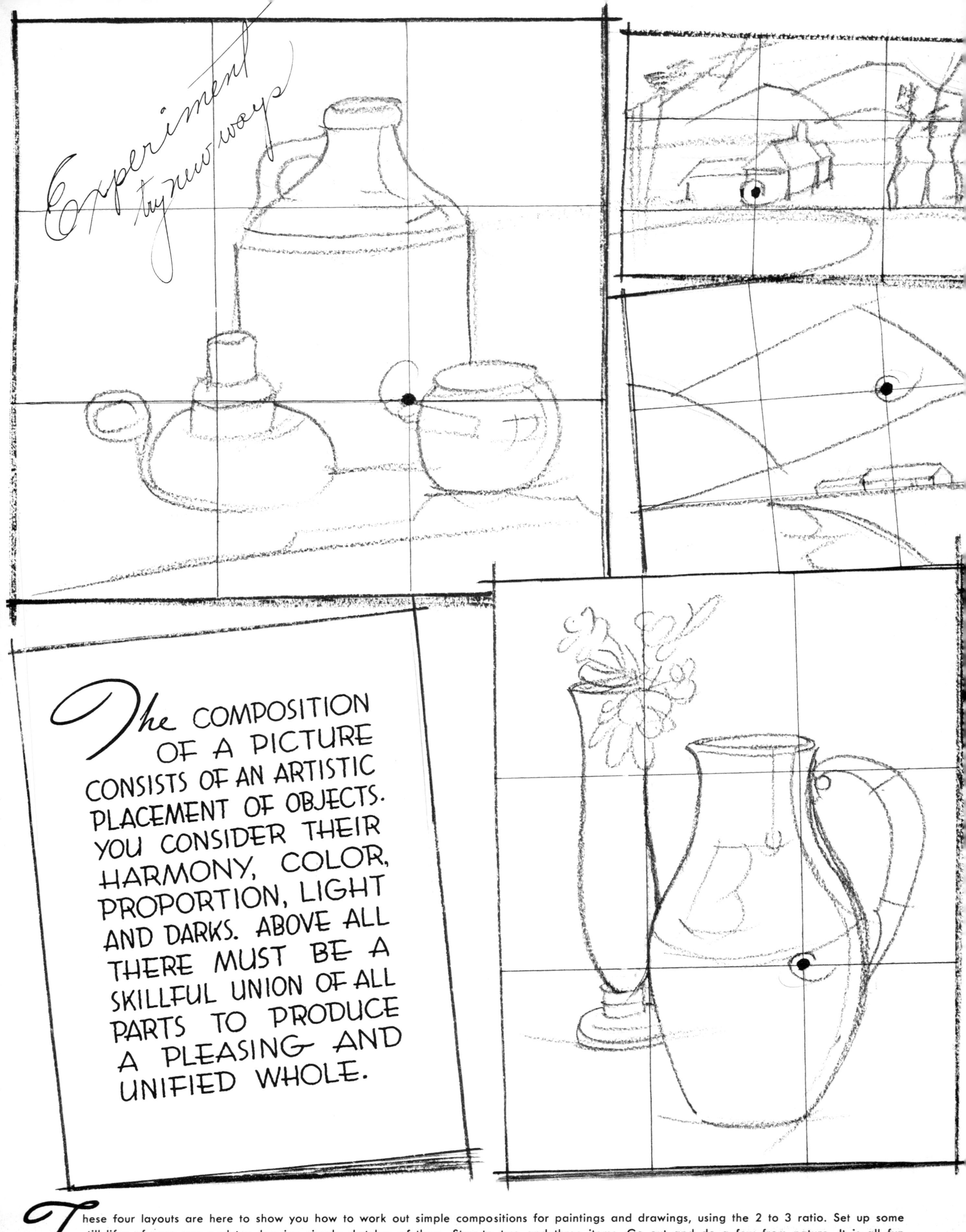

These four layouts are here to show you how to work out simple compositions for paintings and drawings, using the 2 to 3 ratio. Set up some still lifes of your own and try drawing simple sketches of them. Stay to two and three items. Go out and do a few from nature. It is all fun and wonderful practice.

DIRECTIONS

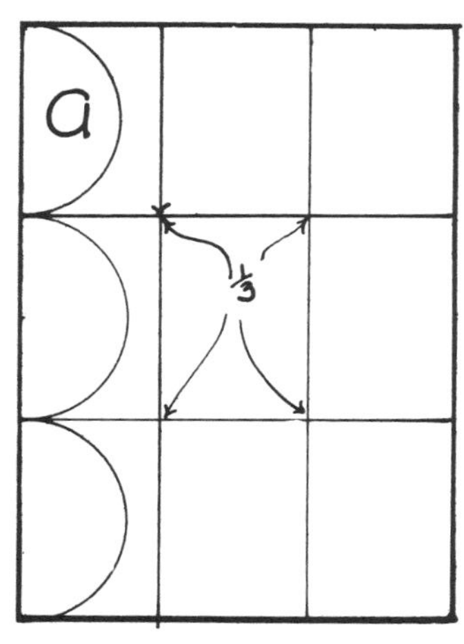

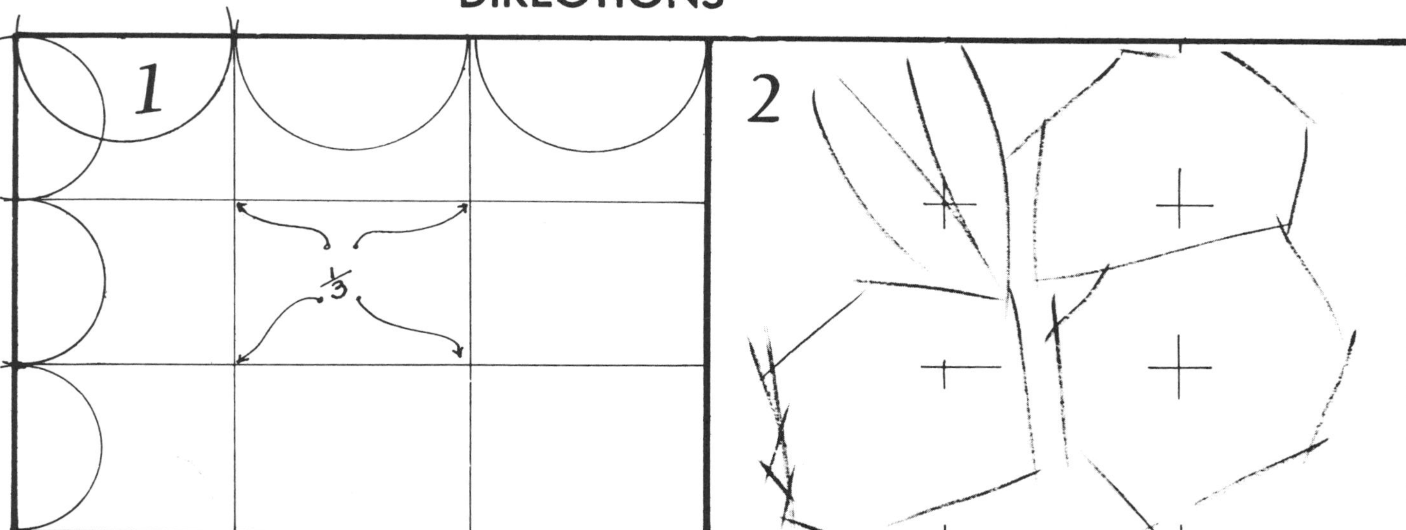

Remember, divide in thirds, decide on the third you wish to place your subject on.

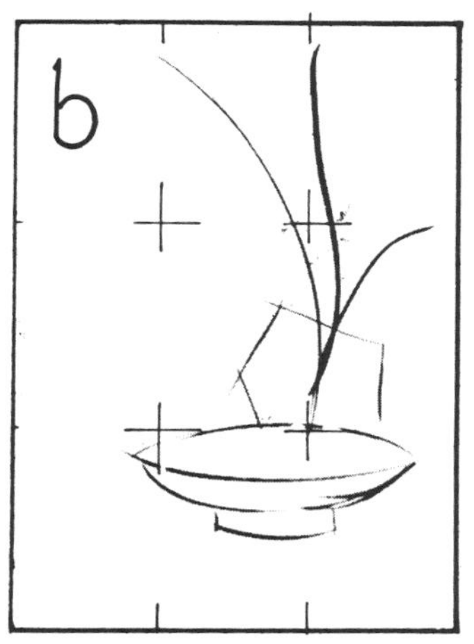

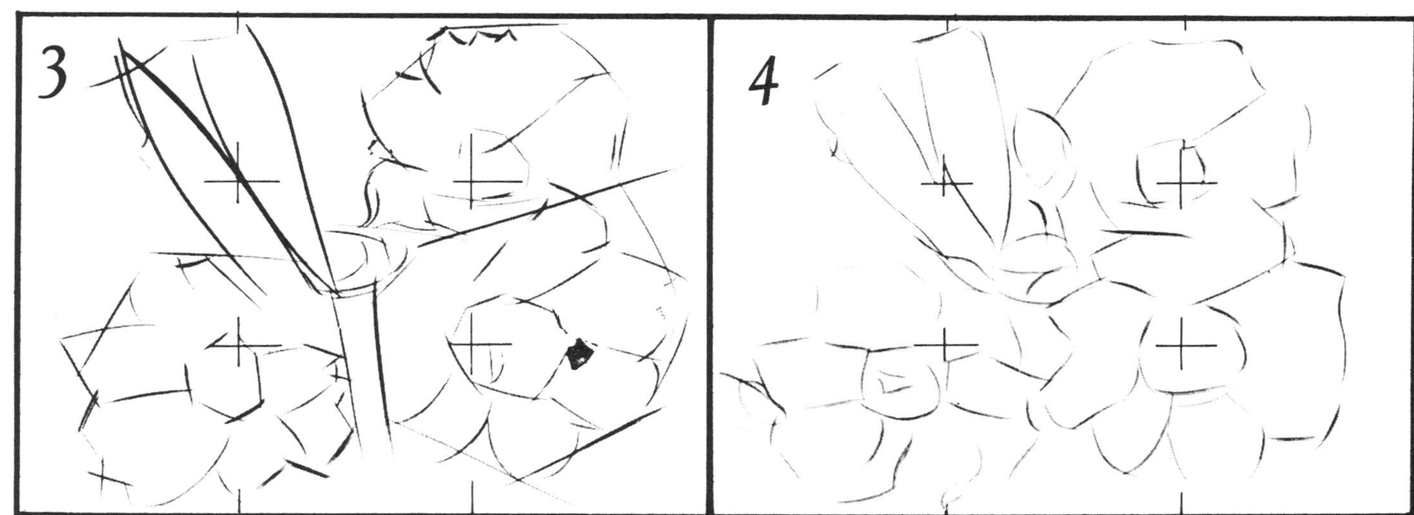

Block in for placement and balance.

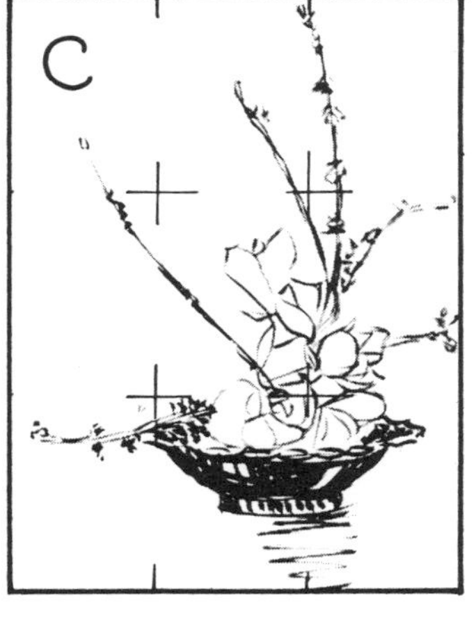

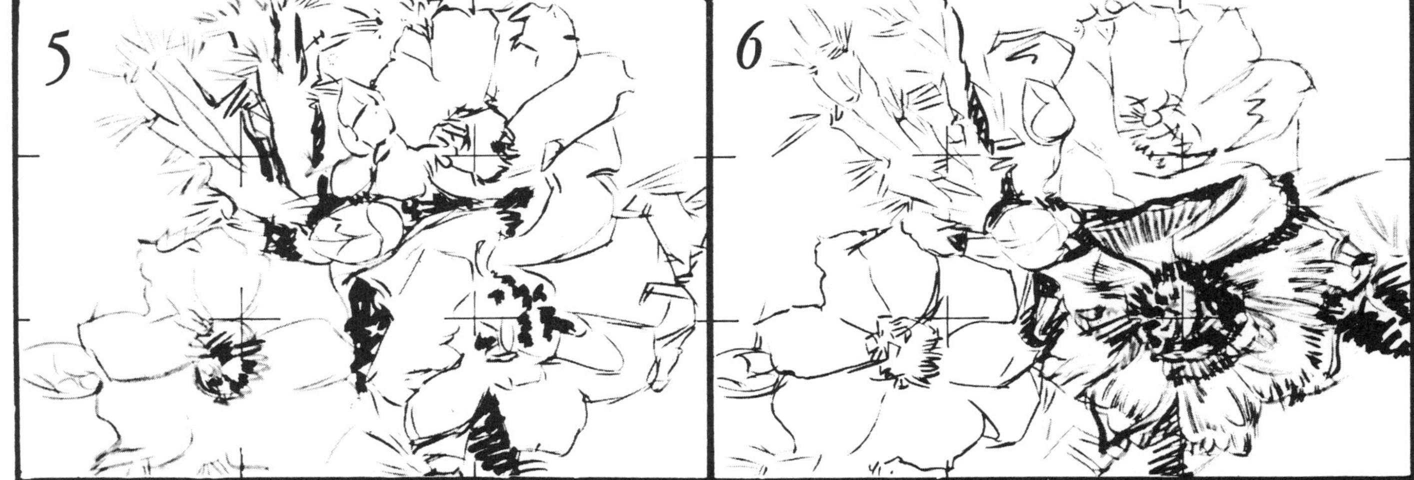

IT IS NOT necessary to center the main object on the one-third mark, but it is all right if you wish to, although it greatly limits your work.

Don't hold to any cut-and-dried rules. Think for yourself and apply what you learn for all sources. After you have placed your main object, all other objects (flowers in this case) become secondary and are placed so they add interest and a background, but must not be made too large or prominent so as to detract from your main object.

There are a number of good books on composition, but I hope to give you a simple way, that may be used with camera, as well as drawing pictures, even just to enjoy others efforts — and you know that is lots of fun. When going into homes, buying pictures for your home, at art galleries, etc., the more you understand, the greater your pleasure. It is NOT a hard job and it becomes quite easy as you keep on trying — and, drawing is a universal language — as I found in a remote part of France on my last trip. We were very hungry and no one in the restaurant spoke English. Our sketchy French along with sign language just confused the proprietor, then it dawned on me DRAWING! So on the back of an envelope, I drew a "T" Bone Steak, and we had a most delicious steak dinner with all the trimmings. One of the party's wrote on the bottom, "Saved from Starvation by this Drawing."

Success and have fun.

Sincerely yours,

W F F

More Ways To Learn...With Walter Foster!

BEGINNERS ART SERIES
Introductory Art Skills

Walter Foster's **Beginners Art Series** is a great way to introduce children to the wonderful world of art. Designed for ages six and up, this innovative instructional series teaches the basics of art and art theory and helps children to develop strong tactile and visual skills. Most importantly, the **Beginners Art Series** makes learning fun! Children will enjoy hours of entertainment with *Drawing Fun, Clay Fun, Color Fun, Paper Art Fun* and each of the

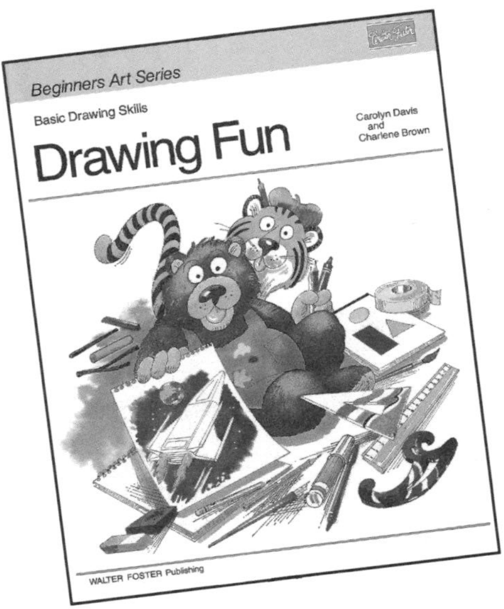

other titles. Written by experts in art education, each book follows a standardized format which includes simple demonstrations with easy to follow instructions, a glossary of art vocabulary, a section discussing materials, and a series of exciting "hands on" projects. Priced to fit every budget, the **Beginners Art Series** is a resource no home or school should be without.

HOW TO SERIES
Developing Art Skills

Walter Foster's **How To Series** can help you become a better artist...easily and economically! This extensive series features art books addressing all media—pencil, watercolor, oil, acrylic, pen & ink, charcoal and pastel—and a variety of subject matter, including animals, cartoons, figures, landscapes, seascapes, and still life. Written

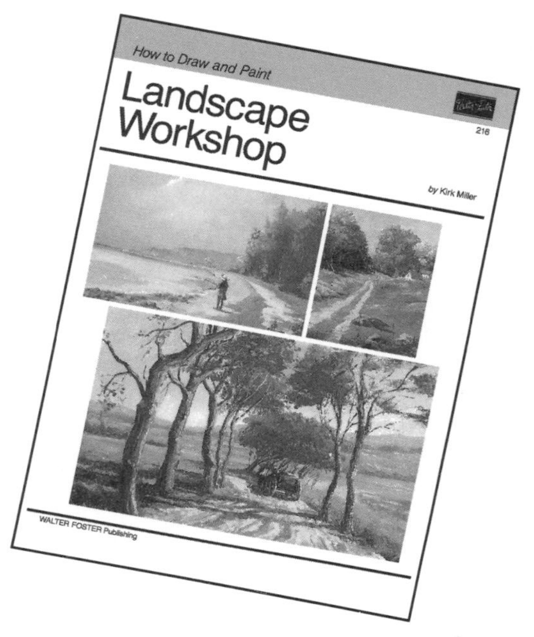

by accomplished artists, the books in the **How To Series** will teach you the basics of form, line and dimension, as well as the intricacies of advanced rendering techniques. You'll learn secrets that have helped our authors achieve excellence in their artistic specialties. There are over 100 titles in the Walter Foster **How To Series.**

ARTIST'S LIBRARY SERIES
Advanced Art Skills

If you're serious about art, then Walter Foster's **Artist's Library Series** is for you! This expanding series offers books addressing a wide variety of mediums, subjects and techniques; ranging from oil painting to watercolors to calligraphy. Each book features step-by-step demonstrations and easy-to-follow instructions. Written by well-

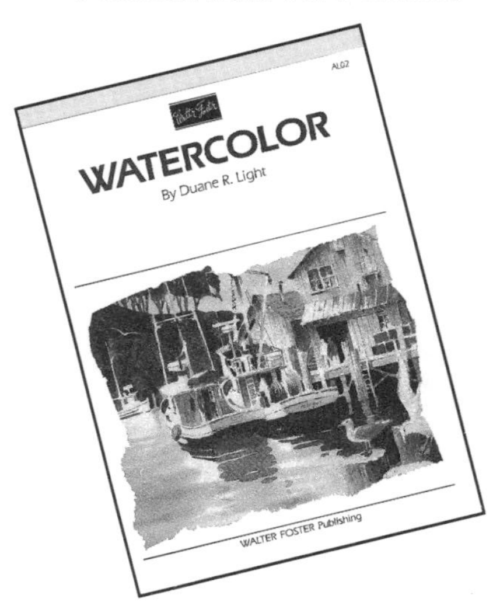

known, highly qualified artists, these books can help you expand your creativity, overcome technical obstacles, or explore new media. Nowhere else will you find such excellent instruction at such a reasonable price. The **Artist's Library Series** is sure to be a welcome addition to your library of art books!